THE BOOK OF
CROWCOMBE, BICKNOLLER and SAMPFORD BRETT

A Portrait of Three Parishes

MAURICE & JOYCE CHIDGEY

First published in Great Britain in 2005

Copyright © 2005 Maurice & Joyce Chidgey

All rights reserved. No part of this publication may be reproduced, stored in a retrieval system, or transmitted in any form or by any means without the prior permission of the copyright holder.

Title page: *Old print of Crowcombe Market Cross.*

British Library Cataloguing-in-Publication Data.
A CIP record for this title is available from the British Library.

ISBN 1 84114 413 4

HALSGROVE

Halsgrove House
Lower Moor Way
Tiverton, Devon EX16 6SS
Tel: 01884 243242
Fax: 01884 243325
E-mail: sales@halsgrove.com
Website: www.halsgrove.com

Printed and bound in Great Britain by CPI Bath.

Whilst every care has been taken to ensure the accuracy of the information contained in this book, the publisher disclaims responsibility for any mistakes which may have been inadvertently included.

FOREWORD

Those of us who live in this part of West Somerset owe a debt of gratitude to Maurice and Joyce Chidgey for all they have done in compiling so interesting and detailed a record of our area and its life during the past and unto the present. To those who have spent all their lives here they give opportunities for enjoying past events again and remembering with pleasure old friends and companions; to the more recent arrivals they offer the chance of being drawn into the lives of their villages and so may, if they wish, become part of them.

Since the Second World War there have been tremendous changes in local life. In broad outline the mechanisation of the farms was possibly the most powerful factor. This did away with the need for so many farm labourers and, as the larger farms normally employed 13 or so, caused a considerable shift in population. Greater ease and speed of travel encouraged many town dwellers to retire to the country and, with the increase and spread of the import trade, the villages no longer needed their self-sufficiency. The village craftsmen – tailors, carpenters, blacksmiths, etc. – became fewer in number. The appearance of the villages changed; poles and wires sprang up everywhere and when it was no longer necessary for each household to grow its own vegetables, lawns and ornamental gardens began to appear. In these circumstances it is clear that some account of the past is very necessary or a great deal of our heritage will be lost.

In this book the deficiency is remedied – the authors have given us a record in picture and word of the changing pattern of life in this neighbourhood, which enables us to see how the village community of the present has evolved and how the solid unity, so valuable at all times, has been preserved.

Vera Yandle
Lifelong resident of Sampford Brett.

Family at Elmfield, Sampford Brett, in late-Victorian times. A young Arthur Jenkins is the driver of the pony trap.

Crowcombe Court, c.1930.

Quantock Moor, Bicknoller, with the former gravel quarry in the background, late 1930s.

CONTENTS

	Foreword	3
	Acknowledgements	7
	Introduction	9
Chapter 1	**Crowcombe**	11
	Crowcombe Court	49
	The Major	53
	Ruth Tongue: Folklorist, Author, Eccentric	54
	Tony Horsey: Distinguished Service and Flying Career	55
	A Crowcombe Childhood	55
	Crowcombe Cricket Club	57
	Coronation Celebrations, 1953	61
	Painting in West Somerset	62
	Extracts from Crowcombe CE School Logbook, 1926–55	64
Chapter 2	**Bicknoller**	75
	Bicknoller Village Hall	102
	Bicknoller's County Cricketers	103
	Two Past Personalities of Bicknoller	104
	Growing Up in Bicknoller	106
	Coronation Celebrations, 1953	109
	Extracts from Bicknoller CE School Logbook, 1881–1900	112
Chapter 3	**Sampford Brett**	117
	Did this Chest Belong to Elizabeth Courtenay?	145
	Vision at the Rectory	146
	The Tailor of Sampford Brett	147
	Early Memories of a Local Bell-Ringer	148
	Coronation Celebrations, 1953	151
	Extracts from Sampford Brett CE School Logbook, 1868–1934	151
	Mothers' Union in the Three Parishes	156
	Subscribers	157
	Further Titles	159

Snowy, the famous white hind of the Quantocks, seen in the midst of other deer. A legend in her own lifetime, she was sadly killed by trophy poachers in 1993 at the age of 19 years. She was held in huge affection locally, and the Quantock Staghounds always steered clear of hunting her.

Thorncombe House, c.1910.

ACKNOWLEDGEMENTS

The purpose of this book is to attempt to portray village life, the ways of this historic countryside and some of the personalities who have added colour to this beautiful area down through the years. We are very appreciative of all the help, kindness and hospitality shown during its compilation, without which publication would not have been possible. Every effort has been made to be accurate using the information received, but we apologise in the event of any errors or omissions. We would like to express our sincere thanks to the present and former people of the three parishes covered, which make up a very special corner of West Somerset, and we hope you enjoy your book!

We gratefully acknowledge the following for the loan of photographs, other material and information: Peter Alcroft and Sharon Murdoch, Richard and Patricia Anderson, Betty Armstrong, Fred Bacon, John Barraclough, Barbara Beer, Olive Birch (the late Peter Birch), Chris Boyles, Chris Brewer, Susan Brooks, David Bulpin, Richard Bulpin, Richard Canever, Michael Chapman, Audrey Chawner, David and Barbara Chidley, Frank Clatworthy collection, the late Mary Croucher, Crowcombe Community Shop, Robin Davies, Gilbert Davis, Anthea Deane, Keith Dickinson, Richard Dinwiddy, Margaret Dunn, Roly Ford, Molly Farmer, Margaret Fountain, John Greswell, Leonard Groves, Steve and Janet Groves, Steve Guscott, George Haller, Joyce Halliday, Diane and Chris Hayes, Jack Henson, Phyllis Herniman, David Hodge, Mrs Horn, Tony Horsey DFM, Joan Hugan, Audrey Hunt, John Jenkins, Margaret Jenkins, Geoff King, Winifred Kingsbury, Brenda Knight, Walter Langdon, Eddie Lawrence, Norah Linck, David Luckett, Mary Maine, Janet Marke, Marie Milnes, Robin and Patricia Murchie, Mary and Stuart Parkman, Tina Pendray, Leslie Pike, Margaret Pumphrey, Margaret and John Reed, Valerie Richards, Nigel Ridler, Mary Rhodes, Pauline Rook, Robin Rutt, Sue Rutt, Sampford Brett History and Archives Group, Martin Southwood, Duncan Stafford, Peter Stradling, David Sully, Haydn Sully, Ann Sweetland, Keith Towells, Julia Tremlett, Clifford Trickey, Anthony Trollope-Bellew, Celia Vardy, Wendy Venner, Margaret Voss, Barry Watkin, Ethel Welsher, Beryl Willes, Michael Williams, Marion Winn, Doreen Woodward, David Worthy, Robert Yandle.

Special thanks for assistance are due to Liz Blazey, Vivian and Anita Brewer, Jeff and June Duddridge, Jean Greswell, Daphne Trollope-Bellew and Vera Yandle. Thanks also to the editor of the *West Somerset Free Press* and the Somerset Record Office.

One map is reproduced from the *Victoria County History, Somerset Volume V*, p55, by permission of the Executive Editor, and two maps by permission of Ordnance Survey.

Lastly, we extend our grateful thanks to Katy Charge, Commissioning Editor of the Halsgrove Community History Series, for her advice and help.

Maurice and Joyce Chidgey, 2005

The yew tree, which at one time grew on the top of Bicknoller Church tower from seed sown by a bird. It was a matter of considerable pride to the village.

Sampford Brett, 1904.

Whortleberry pickers on the Quantocks in the early 1900s. Many families did this to supplement their incomes.

INTRODUCTION

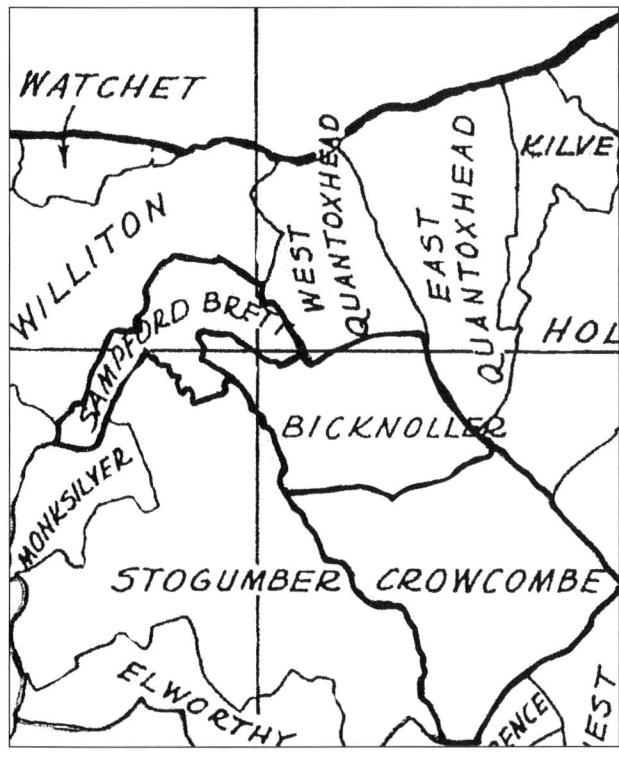

The parishes of Crowcombe, Bicknoller and Sampford Brett are, as for long past, primarily focussed on agriculture, but are also much sought after as retirement havens. Crowcombe and Bicknoller nestle under the western side of the 38 square miles of the Quantock Hills, which were designated an Area of Outstanding Natural Beauty in 1957, the first area in England to be so named. Sampford Brett lies between the Quantock and Brendon Hills in a sheltered position about a mile south of Williton.

Tourism also figures prominently in this area, the Quantocks attracting many visitors with their magnificent views overlooking the Bristol Channel and surrounding countryside, and boasting many beautiful walks. The wild red deer inhabit the Quantocks, along with foxes, badgers and many other mammals which roam amongst the heather and whortleberry bushes; there is also abundant bird life. When in bloom the rhododendrons which grow there are also a delightful sight but suffocating by nature, stifling all else in their path. The magnificent church towers and carved furnishings, notably screens and bench-ends, are among the great glories of West Somerset and are a feature of these three parishes. There are also historic mansions, houses and families, good inns, many farms, characters, artistic craftsmanship, artists and old tales. Among the communal achievements over the years have been the village halls at Bicknoller and Sampford Brett and, more recently, the shops and Post Offices at Bicknoller and Crowcombe and the fine new Crowcombe Hall, which prides itself on a wide range of sport and leisure amenities.

Ecclesiastically, the three parishes form part of the Quantock Towers Benefice, which comprises Bicknoller, Crowcombe, Monksilver, Nettlecombe, Sampford Brett, Stogumber and Elworthy (redundant). The rector of the benefice is the Revd Elfrida Savigear, whose rectory is at Bicknoller. Civically, all three parishes fall within West Somerset District, and had a total population in 2002 of 1,200. The only remaining functional school within the three parishes is at Crowcombe, which still flourishes with a healthy number of pupils engaging in a wide range of activities.

The Revd Elfrida Beatrice Savigear, rector of the Quantock Towers Benefice, in which the three parishes covered in this book form part. She was inducted in February 1999, being the first female priest of the seven parishes in the united benefice.

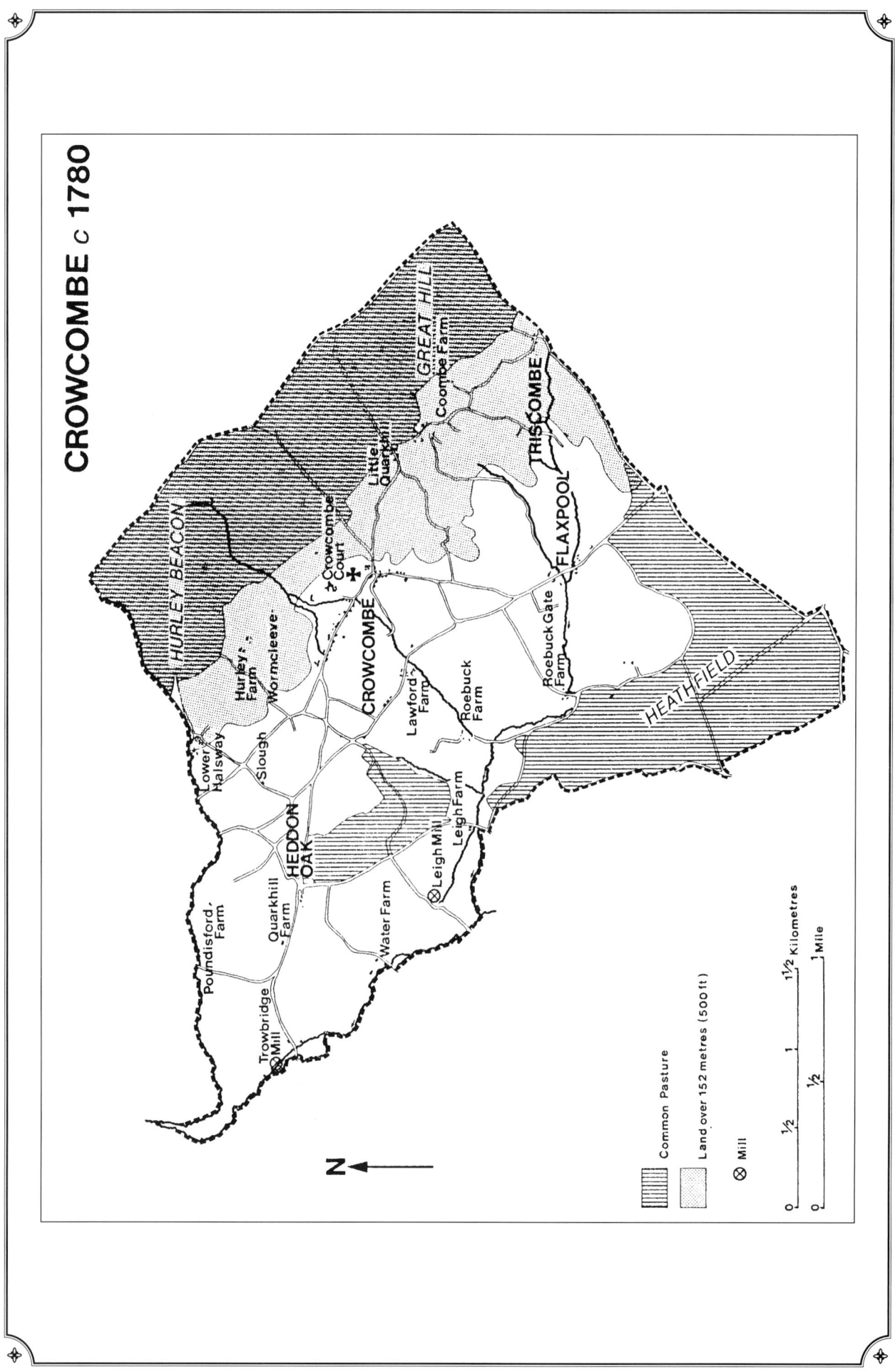

Chapter 1
Crowcombe

Symbolising the essence of the Quantocks is Crowcombe village with the gleaming gem of the Court, near to the gate of which stands the Parish Church with its unusual dedication of Holy Ghost. Directly opposite is a most beautiful Church House. Stretching from the south-west slopes of the Quantocks, with Hurley Beacon, the second highest point on the Quantocks (1,175 feet), in the background and Will's Neck (1,261 feet) in the distance, the parish of Crowcombe – primarily agricultural – reaches from the Quantock ridgeway in the north-east to the upper parts of the Doniford stream, which divides the parish from Stogumber. A stream also divides Crowcombe from Bicknoller, and the boundary crosses the former common of Crowcombe Heathfield and follows a lane and a bank through Triscombe on the south and south-east.

Scattered farmsteads, known in the seventeenth century as villages, may be traced from the thirteenth century, but their origin may be much earlier. In 1267 Water and Leigh are mentioned, Triscombe in 1278, Hurley (Hyerlegh), Cooksley, Roebuck (Ralhock, Rabbock) by 1327, Lawford in 1352, Slough in 1353, Flaxpool in 1355, Wharncliffe (Wormeclyve) in 1360, Combe in 1363, Poundisford (Pouresford) in 1365, Little Quantock in 1391, Roebuck Gate (Mounselyrabbok) in 1415, and Quarkhill by the fifteenth century. Only Cooksley and Combe have not survived, but Cooksley Wood still exists. The farmsteads vary in size and most of the farmhouses were rebuilt during the late-eighteenth century.

From the Quantocks the village is approached from beautiful tree-lined Crowcombe Park Gate down a steep hill from the combe from which it takes its name. Lying in the centre of the parish, it stretches for almost a mile with buildings old and new on each side of the street, known in the eighteenth century as Taunton Street. Over the years some of the old cottages have been demolished and replaced and new housing developments have both enlarged and enhanced the village. Crowcombe once boasted a borough and a market and on a triangle of grass stands a fourteenth-century cross marking the site of an ancient market and fair.

The road through the village, turnpiked by the Minehead Trust in 1807, was then the principal route between Taunton and Watchet. Further west through Lawford there was a secondary route, part of which was adopted when the village was bypassed in 1929.

Combe Road, Crowcombe, in 1937 before it was made up.

General view of Crowcombe at the turn of the last century.

Crowcombe Market Cross in Edwardian times. The old cottages are now demolished.

Crowcombe in the late 1930s. Dick Hill with dog, Ernie Colman with cows and Mr Evans at the forge.

Crowcombe Heathfield railway station, 2003.

The West Somerset Railway has two stations within the parish boundaries – Crowcombe Heathfield and Stogumber. The line was originally laid between Taunton and Watchet in 1862 and run by the Bristol and Exeter Railway, being extended to Minehead in 1874 by the Great Western Railway. Taken over by British Railways in 1947, the line was closed in 1971, but was reopened in 1977 by the new private West Somerset Railway Company. The line now runs from Minehead to Bishops Lydeard, with the company's ultimate aim to have a service into Taunton. In 2004 Crowcombe Heathfield was joint winner of the coveted 'Best Kept Station' award on the line.

The parish had an innkeeper by 1620 and a victualler in 1681. Two inns were later established – The Lion or Three Lions in 1747 (known as the Carew Arms since 1814) and the Railway Inn at Stogumber station in 1894 (closed around 1970). At one time surgeries were held by Dr Meyers' practice in an upstairs room at the Carew Arms. A bowling-green was in the parish in 1733, and from 1812 there was mention of a Stogumber and Crowcombe Benefit Society. Probably founded in 1858, the Crowcombe Friendly Society would hold a feast day on Whit Monday before it was disbanded in 1911.

The Kesteven Recreation Ground was presented to the parish in 1919 by the Honourable Mrs E.M. Trollope in memory of her son, Thomas Carew Trollope, the third Lord Kesteven, who died while on active service in 1915. A memorial to those of the parish who died on active service during the First World War was erected in the far corner of the ground, but was moved to its present site near the Church House in 1969. It bears the names of parishioners who gave their lives in the First World War, also one who died in the Second World War and one who died in a later conflict in Malaya. During the Second World War both British and American troops were stationed near the village and at Crowcombe Heathfield. Both the Recreation Ground and the War Memorial were looked after by the Crowcombe branch of the British Legion (now Royal) when it was formed in 1921, and the branch now covers Crowcombe, Bagborough and Stogumber. The Recreation Ground is now under the jurisdiction of Crowcombe Parish Council and is a fine backcloth for the adjacent magnificent new Crowcombe Hall.

Electricity arrived in the village in 1951, along with a new squire and parson – Major T.F. Trollope-Bellew and the Revd Peter Birkett. The arrival of electricity

CROWCOMBE

The Carew Arms, c.1950.

The War Memorial and Church House, Crowcombe, 2004.

aroused some scepticism, especially among the elderly. One old lady who lived in a thatched cottage thought it would set the thatch alight. However, she did change her mind a little and said: 'I'll switch her on and find the matches to light the lamp'! In those pre-electric days the only lighting was from oil-lamps and candles.

The height of the parish's population was in 1831 when it stood at 691. It was 433 in 1931, 405 in 1951, 434 in 1971, and in 2002 it had risen to 590.

In 854 an estate at 'Cerawicombe' (almost certainly Crowcombe), described as of six hides, was held by Glastonbury Abbey. The manor later came into the possession of the Church, but they lost it before 1086 when it was held under the count of Mortain by Robert, son of Ives, known as Robert the Constable, ancestor of the Beauchamp family. The Beauchamps became tenants in chief on the extinction of the Mortain holding, and the overlordship descended in their family.

Godfrey de Crowcombe was lord of the manor of Crowcombe by 1227 and before his death in 1247 he granted half the manor with the advowson to Studley Priory, Oxfordshire. That half of Crowcombe was known usually as the manor of Crowcombe Studley. The Priory held the estate until its dissolution in 1539, and the Crown sold the manor to John Croke in 1540. He was succeded by his son, Sir John Croke, who conveyed it in 1598 to his sons, John and George. They sold it a year later to Sir George Kingsmill, who passed it on to his nephew, Sir William Kingsmill, and the latter's son, Sir Henry. The manor remained with the Kingsmills until 1789, when Robert Kingsmill sold it to Sir Robert Bateson Harvey, Bt, of Langley Park, Buckinghamshire. The Harveys held the manor for just over 100 years until Sir Robert Greville Harvey sold most of it in 1894 to the Honourable Mrs Ethel Mary Trollope, owner of the other manor in the parish, known as Crowcombe Biccombe or Crowcombe Carew. Thus most of the two halves of Crowcombe were reunited after 650 years.

In the early-thirteenth century part of the village was described as a borough. This was between the Market Cross and Townsend, north-west of the church. The borough was attached to Crowcombe Studley by 1247, but no borough charter survives. There is no evidence of a borough court, but Crowcombe Burgus Court met from 1633–35. The manor of Crowcombe Biccombe held three courts each year in the fourteenth century, decreasing to two by the fifteenth century. The courts appointed a hayward (one who had charge of fences and enclosures and responsibility for ensuring cattle did not stray from common ground), a tithingman and one or sometimes two portreeves. The court was still being held in the Church House in 1876. Crowcombe Studley manor held a court, described as court baron, which met usually once a year in October. A court

The magnificent Crowcombe Hall in its fine setting on the Kesteven Recreation Ground. It was opened in 2003 and has a wide range of sports facilities.

13

book covering the period 1717–42 states that a constable, portreeve and tithingman were elected annually. The constable had responsibility for the repair of the pound, stocks and the armour of the parish. In later years policing at Crowcombe was usually the responsibility of the constable from Stogumber until the 1970s. The repair of the Market Cross in 1724 and the provision of a pillory and stocks up to 1730 were the liability of burgage tenants. In 1894 the borough was conveyed by name with Crowcombe Studley manor, and 'borough' and 'burgage' still survive in field and tenement names.

The first mention of a church and rector in Crowcombe is in 1226, but their presence could very well have been established earlier. The advowson of the rectory was granted by Godfrey de Crowcombe in or before 1247 with his half of the manor to Studley Priory. The patronage descended with the manor of Crowcombe Studley after the Dissolution. The presentation was rarely made by its owners and the Parliamentary Commissioners appointed a rector in 1645. In 1894 the advowson was not sold to the Carews with Crowcombe Studley manor. By 1901 it had been conveyed to Mrs E.M. Young, of Crowcombe House. In that year she presented her son, H.C. Young, who succeeded her, and on his death in 1943 he was followed by his brother and sister, Dr B. Mitchell Young and Miss L. Young, as joint patrons. The advowson was held by them until 1949 when it was transferred to the Bishop of Bath and Wells. From 1975 the living was held with Bicknoller, but now forms part of the Quantock Towers Benefice.

The Parish Church of the Holy Ghost, by which dedication it is known today, having previously been given as Holy Trinity in 1861 and Holy Cross in 1869, is built of local red sandstone with grey stone dressings. The oldest part of the church is the tower, which dates from the fourteenth century. It holds a peal of six bells, the oldest bell dating from about 1440, and also contains a clock. What is unusual about the clock is that it is faceless – it just strikes the hours. It is said that when the clock was installed, agreement could not be reached as to which way it should face. The clock was restored in 1996 in memory of Major T.F. Trollope-Bellew. The tower was originally capped by an 80-foot spire, which was struck by lightning and fell in the afternoon of Sunday 20 December 1724. This caused considerable damage to the church, but fortunately none of the congregation who were sheltering in the porch was injured. Subsequently the top section of the spire was positioned on the north-east corner of the tower where it stayed until 1954 when it was deemed hazardous and was removed to the churchyard where it can still be seen.

Left: *Crowcombe Church when capped by an 80-foot spire.*

Crowcombe Parish Church, 1863. On top of the tower is part of the original spire which was struck by lightning in 1724 and later placed there.

CROWCOMBE

The font at the rear of Crowcombe Church at the turn of the last century. It was moved to its present position in the side chapel in the 1960s.

Left: *Interior of Crowcombe Parish Church, late-nineteenth century. The reredos was carved by Harry Hems, of Exeter, and erected by the Revd T. Boles.*

Left: *Colonel George Henry Warrington Carew, d.1874.*

Right: *The top of Crowcombe Church spire which fell after being struck by lightning in 1/24. It can still be seen in the churchyard.*

Pew ends in Crowcombe Church. The one on the left dates from 1534, the centre one depicts men of Crowcombe tackling the legendary two-headed dragon of Shervage Woods, and the one on the right the Green Man with vines growing from his mouth.

In the main body of the church are a nave and aisle, once known as 'Godfrey de Crowcombe's aisle', and where the font now stands was a medieval chapel. At the west end is a door leading onto a tight spiral stairway giving entrance to a priest's chamber above the south porch. The font stood in this area at one time, with a wall bracket and pulley for raising and lowering the heavy wooden cover. It was then moved to where the organ is now, and later to its present site.

The bench-ends are outstanding, the carvings depicting, among others, the arms of Crowcombe, Biccombe and Carew, the Green Man, and the men of Crowcombe tackling the two-headed dragon of Shervage Woods. The earliest date on the bench-ends is 1534. Several pews were restored in 1892 in memory of Coventry Warrington Carew, who died in 1889.

The north chapel was built by Thomas Carew in 1655 as the manor pew for the family of Crowcombe Court. Known now as the Carew Aisle, it contains hatchments and monuments of the family and is still privately owned. Thomas Parker, architect of Crowcombe Court, made the present screen, rails, altar and pulpit in 1729. On the outside walls of the north chapel are monuments to seven servants of the lords of Crowcombe Carew manor, 1730–1815. The parish registers date from 1641, and the plate includes a paten of 1719, a large flagon of 1729 and a chalice and dish of 1734. Communion was celebrated three or four times a year during the eighteenth century, and by the early-nineteenth century services were held twice on Sundays, with sermons at each. In 1851 a total of 164 people attended morning service and 227 were present at a service in the afternoon.

In 1385 a parsonage house was mentioned, the south front being rebuilt in brick in 1733 after a fire. The building was extended, refitted and re-roofed in the eighteenth and nineteenth centuries, but retained a medieval hall of three bays. In 1976 it was sold and is now two houses known as The Old Rectory and Glebe House.

From 1842–45 private houses were registered for Nonconformist worship, two of them by the Baptist minister from Stogumber. In 1890 a small Baptist chapel was built in the village, but was closed in 1916 – 'there being no nonconformists resident in Crowcombe'. The Somerset Congregational Union bought a site for a chapel in 1921, but it was never built on and the land was sold in 1961.

In 1514 a house and garden opposite the churchyard, jointly held by the lords of the manors of Crowcombe Studley and Crowcombe Biccombe, were granted to a group of parishioners. There was

Crowcombe Rectory before it was made into two houses, c.1863.

Crowcombe Rectory in Edwardian times. It is reputed that the Rectory has been haunted by a lady attired in blue.

a condition that the house should be rebuilt within four years. The new building was known as the Parish or Church House for the purpose of holding church ales (the name given to a feast or revel). It was later used as a poorhouse and a school, but as a workhouse was constructed in Williton in 1838 Crowcombe had no further need of a poorhouse. The school vacated the upper floor in 1872 following the opening of the Church School. The Church House remained empty for the next 30 years, falling into disrepair, although an effort was made in 1897 to restore the building in celebration of Queen Victoria's Diamond Jubilee but the project was abandoned. However, thanks to the initiative and effort of the Revd H. Christian Young (rector of Crowcombe), other clergy and the help of the Charity Commissioners, restoration was started in 1905. An appeal for £500 was launched and restoration was successfully completed in 1908. The first floor became a social room and the ground floor a men's institute and reading-room. During the Second World War the property was requisitioned for an army canteen and dances and concerts were frequently held on the upper floor. Following the war the first floor was used as the Village Hall again, while Somerset County Council Meals Service rented the ground floor where the village schoolchildren took their midday meals.

The three cottages adjoining Church House were demolished in 1963 as part of a road improvement scheme. The east end of Church House and the now-exposed stairway were restored, and further work was carried out in 1981. Although a new Village Hall was opened in 2003, Church House is still used for art exhibitions and other activities.

The parish had a schoolmaster before 1687 and a parish charity school was founded under the will of the Revd Dr Henry James, son of a former rector. This school took four boys and one girl and was opened in 1718, with Thomas Carew paying the schoolmaster from 1730 and adding a further endowment in 1733. The school had 36 boys and six girls in 1759.

The parish had four day schools by 1835 with a total of 97 pupils. Three of the schools were supported by the James and Carew charities, paying for 36 pupils. Voluntary contributions supported a free Sunday school in 1825, with 10 boys and 20 girls attending. There were 57 Sunday-school children at

The old Church House, Crowcombe, c.1895.

The ancient arched beamed roof of Crowcombe Church House, c.1910.

The old Church House after restoration, mostly paid for by public subscription, c.1908.

Church House Cottages, Crowcombe, c.1947. The cottages on the right were demolished in 1963 because of the dangerous corner and the War Memorial resited there.

morning and afternoon services at the Parish Church in 1851. Only one school remained in 1854, with continued support from the two charities. These charities subsequently augmented school funds and the income was spent on school prizes.

From 1872 the day school was linked with the National Society when it was transferred from the Church House to a new building on the southern edge of the village. This was built on land and with money provided by Colonel George Henry Warrington Carew (1830–74). Later an extension was made to the building, which was opened by the Honourable Mrs E.M. Trollope. Further additions and improvements have been made over the years. In 1883 the average attendance was 75, but fell to 55 in 1889. There were 69 children on the books in 1902, but thereafter numbers gradually declined. Children over age 11 travelled to school in Williton from 1948, and from 1971 children left at the age of nine. In 1976 there were 29 children on the books and over recent years numbers have been fairly constant. A pioneering new partnership between Crowcombe and Stogumber Church of England Schools was started in September 2004. Anthea Deane, head of Crowcombe School, also then took on Stogumber School for a one-year trial period. The scheme was backed by the Bath and Wells Dioecese, local education chiefs and both sets of governors. This move was formalised at the start of the new school year in September 2005 when the two schools officially came under the umbrella of a single governing body after deciding to 'federate' to ensure their future viability. Under the new arrangement Mrs Deane formally took over the reins as head teacher of both schools. In 2005 Crowcombe had 31 pupils and Stogumber 24. By federating, the schools will be able to take part in joint activities and share teaching expertise, and it is to be hoped that both schools remain open for many years to come.

A boarding-school run by John Tucker was transferred from Cannington to Crowcombe in 1789, and may have occupied Timewell Cottage and its neighbour. Crowcombe Court was occupied by Brympton School, an independent boys' boarding-school formerly at Brympton d'Evercy, from 1974–76.

Small plots of common on the Quantocks were ploughed by 1405 and parts of the commons at Heddon and Heathfield by the 1430s for growing rye.

Leigh Mill farmhouse.

CROWCOMBE

The Steyning family held Grimes Farm as a freehold of Crowcombe Studley manor from 1462 until the seventeenth century. Seven tenements were combined and a new farmhouse built to create a holding of 120 acres in 1767. At Hurley in 1777 a new farmhouse was built, around which a farm of 119 acres was formed in 1791. Several tenements were united at Flaxpool with part of the manor farm and a further farm was added in 1793 to create a holding of 425 acres, the largest in the parish. A new farmhouse built there in 1789 was expensively altered in 1793 and for a time was called Norfolk Farm (a farmer from Norfolk having settled there).

Under an Act of 1776, the commons at Heddon and Crowcombe Heathfield and part of that on the Quantocks, 600 acres in all, were enclosed in 1780. By 1791 nearly half the enclosed land was in tillage and part of Heddon Common was planted with wood. In 1842 the Biccombe estate was 1,418 acres and the Studley estate 1,382 acres, the largest farms being Hurley (253 acres) and Little Quantock (335 acres). The only large freeholds were Heathfield (335 acres), created from former common, the Glebe (63 acres), Slades (57 acres), and Brewers Water with Grimes (49 acres).

Dairying had increased sharply by 1976 with 84 per cent of the farmland under grass. There were well over 1,000 cows at that time compared with only 60 in 1828, but at the time of writing the number had decreased considerably. In the latter part of the twentieth century there was a specialist fruit farm at Quarkhill, now gone.

In the seventeenth century weavers, a dyer and a woolcomber were active, and clothier Robert Pyke was prosecuted in 1631 for not pressing his cloth. Bark from the woodlands supplied tanners in the seventeenth century, a tanhouse at Leigh was mentioned in 1741, and there was an extensive tanyard behind Timewell Cottage in 1842. By 1513 a quarry had been opened, later to be followed by a red sandstone quarry at Lawford and a limestone quarry at Townsend Lane. There were further quarries at Halsway, Little Quantock and Triscombe. In 1836 a horse breaker was recorded, by 1839 a grocer and ironmonger had opened a shop, and there was a surgeon in 1843 and a veterinary surgeon in 1859. There were two road contractors and a coal dealer in 1897 and a cattle food agent in 1914, followed by a saddlery and a butcher's shop.

The right to hold a weekly market on Fridays and an annual fair on the eve, day and morrow of All Saints (31 October to 2 November) was granted to Godfrey de Crowcombe in 1227. The market day was altered to Monday in 1230. After the market and fair had been discontinued for some time, the market was revived by Thomas Carew in 1764. He provided stalls for butchers and bakers and tubs for corn and fruit free of charge. The fair was revived in 1767 and another established on the first Friday in May, mainly for the sale of cattle and drapery. The market had ceased by 1791, although the October fair continued. In 1799 a market house adjoining the Carew Arms was converted to a stable for the inn. No later reference to either a fair or market has been discovered. The site of the medieval market is probably marked by the fourteenth-century cross at the south-eastern end of the borough.

Leigh Mill is one of the earliest mentioned in Crowcombe. Forming part of Crowcombe Biccombe manor, it was leased from 1353 for the rent of one bushel of corn a week. In 1641 the mill was held with a hop yard and a wood above the millpond. In 1778 the mill and mill house were destroyed by fire, the property being rebuilt by a Stogumber miller by 1780 and renamed New Mill. By 1875 the mill had apparently ceased to grind. It has long since been demolished, but the mill house, leat and pond (now both waterless) still survive under the name of Leigh Mill Farm. Other mills also existed in the parish.

With Crowcombe situated in the centre of the Quantocks it can reasonably claim to be the focal point of the Quantock Staghounds. Initially the Quantocks were hunted as part of the hunt country of the Devon and Somerset Staghounds. The Quantock Staghounds were formed in 1902 by Mr E.V. Stanley, of Quantock Lodge. They were hunted by him until 1907 when they were disbanded, but were restarted in 1917 under the mastership of Col Dennis Boles, with the help of the Government and the Quantock country being hunted by courtesy of the Devon and Somerset Staghounds. At the time of writing, hunting is facing significant changes following the Parliamentary ban on hunting with dogs, which came into force during February, 2005.

In local government the parish joined Williton Poor Law Union in 1836, from 1894 was part of Williton Rural District, and has been in West Somerset District since 1974. Crowcombe has a Parish Council.

Over the years there were various charities for the poor of the parish, but these are now defunct except for the Carew and James charities, which supports Crowcombe School.

Vivian Brewer, Crowcombe's representative on West Somerset District Council. At the time of writing he has so far served on the authority for 29 years, with two terms as chairman.

Opening of the new village Post Office and shop

The opening ceremony at Crowcombe's new village shop and Post Office, April 2001. Among those present were Mrs Mary Rhodes, great-granddaughter of Crowcombe shopkeeper Charles Jordan back in 1871, and Mrs Ethel Welsher, the village's oldest inhabitant. The former Post Office had closed just over a year earlier when sub-postmaster Viv Brewer retired. The new venture was brought to fruition by determined villagers joining together to form Crowcombe Village Shop Association – a non-profit-making friendly society with private shareholders who gave interest-free loans. A key player was local landowner Daphne Trollope-Bellew, who generously leased an old barn called Rapps to convert into the Post Office and store. Grants were given by Somerset County Council, West Somerset District Council, Somerset Community Council, the Quantock Hills Joint Advisory Committee and the Regional Development Agency. The new sub-postmaster is Mr Joe Butterworth. Left to right, foreground: Mrs Mary Rhodes, Mrs Sarah Baker with Max (youngest Crowcombe inhabitant) and Beth, Joe Butterworth (sub-postmaster), Mrs Ethel Welsher (oldest inhabitant), Mrs Daphne Trollope-Bellew with Harriet Trollope-Bellew.

Official opening of the new Crowcombe Hall

Villagers and guests celebrate the official opening of Crowcombe Hall in March 2003, by local county councillor Anthony Trollope-Bellew. It is built on the site of the former cricket pavilion on the Kesteven Recreation Ground, and there are good parking facilities. The hall boasts a wide range of sport and leisure activities, including facilities for badminton, five-a-side football, indoor cricket, short mat bowls, a youth club, amateur dramatics, etc. It is also ideal for dances, concerts, weddings, birthday and anniversary celebrations, jumble sales, whist drives and parish meetings. Adjacent to the main hall are two changing rooms complete with showers, used primarily by the cricket and other sports clubs. The Quantock Room is a largely self-contained suite to cater for smaller functions and groups. There is also a fully equipped kitchen, toilets and baby-changing facilities. The National Lottery contributed £267,995 towards the cost of the £364,595 scheme, while county, district and parish councils pledged a further £52,100. That left villagers the daunting task of finding the remaining £45,000 themselves – which they did through donations, fund-raising events and a celebrity auction. The hall is a splendid asset and is designed to meet the many and varied needs of Crowcombe and the surrounding community.

Amateur dramatics

The cast of Everyman, *a play produced by the Revd Peter Birkett in Crowcombe Church in the late 1950s. Among those pictured are: Edward Llewellyn St John Couch, Revd Peter Birkett, June Duddridge, Winifred Jordan, Mrs T. Webber, Major and Mrs Jessop, Sylvia Stevens, Dorcas Lewis, Phyllis Powe, Dr Heineman and Millie Chidley.*

Cast of Ruth Tongue's production of The Bluebird *at Crowcombe in 1962.*

A village Shakespearean production, c.1960s.

A Crowcombe concert group, c.1960s.

Royal British Legion

British Legion standard bearers at a Legion fête at Crowcombe Court in the 1960s. Left to right: Walter Welsher, Albert Welsher, Fred Berryman (chairman), ?, Ethel Routley.

Long service awards for Crowcombe poppy sellers, 1999. Left to right: Joan Sweeney, ?, Lady Bunbury, Ethel Welsher; front: Les Pike.

Mrs Ethel Welsher proudly holding her medal with gold bar presented to her by the Royal British Legion in honour of her 50 years' service as a poppy seller. Mrs Welsher has been a Legion member since 1946 and at the time of writing is Crowcombe's oldest resident, having attained the age of 97 years.

David Emery (right), standard-bearer, Crowcombe and District Branch Royal British Legion, 1995.

Les Pike (chairman) cutting the cake to celebrate the 50th anniversary of Crowcombe and District Royal British Legion in 1971.

Parish and People

James Grant, of Timewell, Crowcombe, with his great-granddaughter Queenie Ash, aged six (later to become Mrs Payne), 1914.

Right: Flag-bearers Albert Welsher and his grandson Reg Colman celebrating the Coronation of King George VI, 1937.

A parade in celebration of the Coronation of King George VI, 1937.

Sir Alexander Acland-Hood, Bt, making a speech to a Primrose League (Conservative) gathering at Crowcombe Court, 1905.

Crowcombe Friendly Society, 1891.

Crowcombe football team in the late 1920s. Left to right, back row: Cyril Lock, Harry Smith, ?, Jim Merson, Fred Smith, Bill Payne, Ted Dinwiddy, ?, Jim Harris, Revd C. Young; middle: F. Westcott, Bert Durrant, Bill Walford; front: Ted Merson, George Radford, Steve Duddridge.

An athletic event at Crowcombe in Edwardian times.

Mrs Ethel Welsher planting the millennium oak on the Kesteven Recreation Ground.

Crowcombe Women's Institute at Rexton Gorse, c.1950. Among those present are: Mrs Hill, Mrs Cooper, Mrs F. Smith, Mrs Strong, Mrs Long, Mrs Bex, Mrs H. Smith, Mrs Bell, Mrs Thompson, Mrs Woolston-Smith, Mrs Kelland, Mrs Chidley, Miss Chidley, Mrs Ash, Mrs Duddridge, Miss Cochram, Miss Follett, Miss D. Follett, Mrs Lovelace.

CROWCOMBE

Sarah Smith in her pony and trap delivering milk at Crowcombe in the 1920s.

Above: *Newly-built council-houses (left) at Crowcombe, c.1955.*

Left: *Crowcombe Women's Institute outing in Jennings' charabanc, c.1925.*

Yeomanry camp at Crowcombe, 1905.

Crowcombe folk dancers, c.1925. Left to right, back row: Ethel Merson, Margaret Govier, Nance Gadd; front: ? Bennett, Norma Boyles, Lizzie Duddridge.

Crowcombe lord of the manor Anthony Trollope-Bellew and his wife Annabel with their daughters Emma (left) and Harriet on the occasion of Anthony's 50th birthday, 2003. Anthony farms Hurley Farm and is also county councillor for the Watchet and Quantocks Division, of which Crowcombe, Bicknoller and Sampford Brett are part.

A trip to the seaside in the 1920s. Left to right: Mrs Tozer, Mrs Kelland, Mrs Jennings, Miss Carew.

Warren's butcher's van stranded in a deep snowdrift at Seven Ash, 1962–63. It was there for three days full of meat, which remained quite edible as it was completely frozen.

At Crowcombe crossroads, c.1930s. The man holding the horse is Ted Hunt.

CROWCOMBE

Crowcombe, showing Jordan's shop on the right.

Wedding of Maurice Jordan and Edith Morgan, c.1906. On the far left is Charles Jordan, who built the shop at Crowcombe which opened in 1871.

Below: *Members of the Jordan family in fancy dress at Crowcombe in the 1950s. Left to right: Hazel, Pyne, Lavinia and Susan* (in front).

Back row: *Leslie Jordan, Winifred Adams (district nurse, later to become Mrs Leslie Jordan);* front: *Edith Jordan, Alice Adams, c.1940.*

Heddon Oak, Crowcombe, from which it is reputed that two Stogumber men were hanged in 1685 for their part in the Monmouth Rebellion. The tree was felled in 1980 as it was deemed to be in a dangerous condition. However, after it was felled it was discovered from its rings that it was too young to have stood at the time of the Bloody Assize. Of course, the men could have been hung from an earlier tree which had died and been replaced by this one.

Timewell Cottage after the fire in 2000.

Timewell Cottage, Crowcombe.

Vivian Brewer with his wife Anita on his retirement and closure of the Post Office at Southleigh, Crowcombe, in March 2000. The Post Office was moved to Southleigh in 1960, when it was run by Vivian's mother, Mrs Lilian Brewer, then by Mary Brewer, followed by Vivian.

Lifelong friends Tom Knell and Tom Savage, left and right of the banner, at Crowcombe at the end of their 252-mile sponsored trek to raise money for the NSPCC in Somerset and the children's unit at Musgrove Park Hospital, Taunton, in 2000. After 19 days on the South West Coastal Path, from Land's End they learnt they had reached their target of £2,000, and were given a great welcome home by family, friends and villagers, Vivian Brewer (chairman of West Somerset District Council) and Charlotte Grayson (NSPCC area appeals manager).

CROWCOMBE

Crowcombe, showing Jordan's shop on the right.

Wedding of Maurice Jordan and Edith Morgan, c.1906. On the far left is Charles Jordan, who built the shop at Crowcombe which opened in 1871.

Below: *Members of the Jordan family in fancy dress at Crowcombe in the 1950s. Left to right:* Hazel, Pyne, Lavinia and Susan *(in front).*

Back row: *Leslie Jordan, Winifred Adams (district nurse, later to become Mrs Leslie Jordan);* front: *Edith Jordan, Alice Adams, c.1940.*

Chris Hayes, BA (Hons), garden designer, with the Vellacott Cup and Perpetual Cup for champion of Crowcombe Flower Show, 2004.

Crowcombe Christmas Club, 2000. Left to right, back row: Bev Cunliffe, Di Rexworthy, Curly Rexworthy, Helen Hatfield, Philippa Staniland, Mary Jane Baker; front: Annabel Trollope-Bellew, Daphne Trollope-Bellew, Margaret Kennington, Barbara Chidley, Joan Hurd.

Rose Cottage, Crowcombe, in Edwardian times.

The Blue Ball Inn, Triscombe, 2004.

How we used to cook – an old kitchen range found at The Cottage (now Hooks).

The Cottage (now known as Hooks), Crowcombe.

CROWCOMBE

Crowcombe, showing Jordan's shop on the right.

Wedding of Maurice Jordan and Edith Morgan, c.1906. On the far left is Charles Jordan, who built the shop at Crowcombe which opened in 1871.

Below: *Members of the Jordan family in fancy dress at Crowcombe in the 1950s. Left to right:* Hazel, Pyne, Lavinia *and* Susan *(in front).*

Back row: *Leslie Jordan, Winifred Adams (district nurse, later to become Mrs Leslie Jordan);* front: *Edith Jordan, Alice Adams, c.1940.*

Chris Hayes, BA (Hons), garden designer, with the Vellacott Cup and Perpetual Cup for champion of Crowcombe Flower Show, 2004.

Crowcombe Christmas Club, 2000. Left to right, back row: Bev Cunliffe, Di Rexworthy, Curly Rexworthy, Helen Hatfield, Philippa Staniland, Mary Jane Baker; front: Annabel Trollope-Bellew, Daphne Trollope-Bellew, Margaret Kennington, Barbara Chidley, Joan Hurd.

Rose Cottage, Crowcombe, in Edwardian times.

The Blue Ball Inn, Triscombe, 2004.

How we used to cook – an old kitchen range found at The Cottage (now Hooks).

The Cottage (now known as Hooks), Crowcombe.

CROWCOMBE

Crowcombe House, built in 1739, one of the finest houses of its period in the area.

Croquet on the lawns of Crowcombe House in Edwardian times.

Crowcombe Post Office when it was at Newton Cottage, c.1905.

Crowcombe, c.1912, showing the old saddlery shop on the right.

Combe Cottage, Crowcombe, c.1920.

The Homestead (now partially demolished), Flaxpool.

Flaxpool Hill, Crowcombe, c.1930.

CROWCOMBE

The Crowcombe bell-ringers being entertained at Flaxpool Farm by Mr and Mrs Clifford Henson, c.1951. Left to right, front: Mrs Birkett, Clifford Henson, Mrs Henson; some of the others pictured: Harry Smith, Wilf Chidley, Amy Duddridge, Ern Colman, Leonard Richards, Albert Welsher, Cyril Ash, Revd Peter Birkett.

Pair of cruets presented to the Church of the Holy Ghost, Crowcombe, by Mrs Henson and inscribed: 'To the glory of God and in memory of Clifford J. Henson, churchwarden of this parish 1936–52'.

Lawford Cottage after the fire. It was rebuilt and renamed Merson's Cottage.

Lawford Cottage before it was destroyed by fire in 1929; it was then occupied by John Merson and family.

The ford (the water now flows under the road) at Lawford, c.1930.

Gathering wood in a putt cart at Combe Hill, c.1900.

31

Heddon Oak, Crowcombe, from which it is reputed that two Stogumber men were hanged in 1685 for their part in the Monmouth Rebellion. The tree was felled in 1980 as it was deemed to be in a dangerous condition. However, after it was felled it was discovered from its rings that it was too young to have stood at the time of the Bloody Assize. Of course, the men could have been hung from an earlier tree which had died and been replaced by this one.

Timewell Cottage after the fire in 2000.

Timewell Cottage, Crowcombe.

Vivian Brewer with his wife Anita on his retirement and closure of the Post Office at Southleigh, Crowcombe, in March 2000. The Post Office was moved to Southleigh in 1960, when it was run by Vivian's mother, Mrs Lilian Brewer, then by Mary Brewer, followed by Vivian.

Lifelong friends Tom Knell and Tom Savage, left and right of the banner, at Crowcombe at the end of their 252-mile sponsored trek to raise money for the NSPCC in Somerset and the children's unit at Musgrove Park Hospital, Taunton, in 2000. After 19 days on the South West Coastal Path, from Land's End they learnt they had reached their target of £2,000, and were given a great welcome home by family, friends and villagers, Vivian Brewer (chairman of West Somerset District Council) and Charlotte Grayson (NSPCC area appeals manager).

CROWCOMBE

The Trollope-Bellew family 'doing their bit' in 1941. Left to right, back row: Anthony F., Major Thomas F.; front: Colonel Froud, Nesta.

Jack (left) and Jim Henson in Home Guard uniform, c.1942.

Crowcombe and District Home Guard, early 1940s. Left to right, back row: ?, Pte O'Shea, ?, Bert Durrant, ?; middle: William Payne, Herbert Herniman, ?, George Touchin, ?, Bill Chidley, Roy Baker, ?, Pte Cooper, Pte Smith, ?; front: Bill Parsons (on motorcycle), Jim Henson, ?, Stan Taylor, Sergt Mallett, Col Hewlett, Jim Merson, Bill Tuckfield, ?, Arthur Hall.

Wild red deer on the Quantocks above Crowcombe.

Rick-making at Brewers Water Farm, c.1947. Left to right, top: ?, Stella Seamark, Les Pike, Agnes Pike, ? Moon; middle: Kathleen Massey; front: ?, Nellie Pike, Bob Massey, Tom Yeandle.

Left to right: *Jim, Nellie and Les Pike, Mary (Polly) Bucknall, c.1942.*

Les Pike at the wheel of a Fordson Major tractor, c.1948.

Haymaking time at Brewers Water Farm, c.1946. Les Pike is on top of the hay with, left to right: Mary Sargent, Agnes Pike, ?.

Les Pike with working horses, Smart, Captain and Prince, c.1946.

Les Pike with a two-furrow plough which was used on steep land and pulled by three horses. The plough has been in the Pike family for over a century and was on exhibition at Crowcombe in 1980.

CROWCOMBE

Left: *A young Jack Henson milking a cow at Flaxpool Farm in the early 1930s.*

Below: *Cottages (now demolished) at Flaxpool, c.1920.*

Florence (left) *and Clifford Henson, c.1930. The lady in the centre is unknown.*

Walter Gibbs (holding the horse), *with Jack and Clifford Henson at Flaxpool Farm, 1932.*

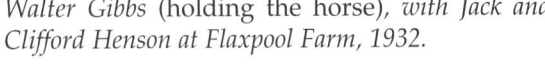

Rose Cottages, next door to the Carew Arms, Crowcombe, 1910.

Beadons, Crowcombe, c.1920.

The Rookery, Crowcombe (now demolished), c.1957.

Stephen Duddridge painting a ladder which he made years previously, c.1952.

Crowcombe craftsman Jeff Duddridge at the 250-year-old bench used by his great-grandfather.

The case of this grandfather clock was made by Jeff Duddridge from timber of the Heddon Oak.

Studying the plans for the building of a new bungalow at Crowcombe Heathfield, 1949. Left to right: Harry and Hector Potter, Frank Webber, Jeff and Stephen Duddridge.

CROWCOMBE

Paul Duddridge (bending over) *and Brian Gibbs looking into a pond built by the Revd Peter Birkett in the Rectory garden at Crowcombe in the 1960s.*

Cyril Lock, a former well-known Crowcombe personality and landlord of the Carew Arms.

Cyril Lock at the wheel of his Austin car which he also used as a taxi in the 1930/40s.

The Rexworthy children, c.1957: Sylvia (back) *with, left to right, Barbara, Christopher and Peter.*

Wilfred Chidley astride his AJS motorcycle, 1947. Wilfred was tower captain of Crowcombe Parish Church bell-ringers for many years.

Frank Chidley racking hay at Water Farm, 1930.

Frank Chidley busy at Water Farm, 1948.

Wilf Chidley with Fordson Major tractor, seed trailer and Massey-Harris corn drift at Water Farm, 1949.

An aerial view of Water Farm, 1965.

CROWCOMBE

Master thatcher Bill Horsey, of Crowcombe, preparing for a stint at his craft. Bill, who was always known as 'Corporal', was also Crowcombe's barber – a task he usually carried out on Sunday mornings. Amateur dramatics was another of his interests and he also appeared in local concerts. His ornamental thatching work has been featured in books and magazines, and he once went, reluctantly, to Pinewood Studios to thatch a house on a film set. After completing this he was asked to go to the USA to do some thatching, but refused. Years later he unfortunately had a fall from a roof he was thatching and this had a bearing upon his death.

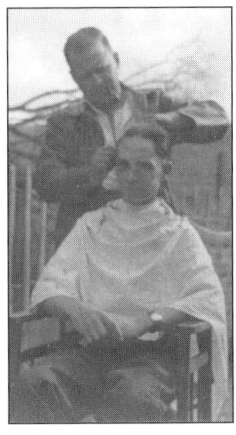

Demon Barber of Crowcombe, Bill 'Corporal' Horsey, with one of his 'victims', c.1960.

Right: *Bill 'Corporal' Horsey busy thatching a roof in the 1950s.*

Pound Orchard with Crowcombe Parish Church in the background.

One of the former Hagley Cottages (now demolished) at Crowcombe.

Stogumber railway station, c.1914.

Quantock Abbey Wine Cellars (formerly the old piggery), Crowcombe, 2004.

Mr Bailey walking behind two cows; Sarah Smith is in front with the pony and trap delivering milk at Crowcombe in 1933.

CROWCOMBE

Decorative arches at Crowcombe in celebration of Queen Victoria's Golden Jubilee, 1887.

Edwin Hunt with a shire horse at the stable yard, Crowcombe Court, c.1914.

Maypole dancing at Crowcombe in the mid-1950s.

The Revd Peter Birkett and assistant at a coster barrow market in the stable yard of Crowcombe Rectory in the late 1950s.

Three young señoritas at the Crowcombe coster market in the late 1950s. Left to right: Rosemary Cavill, Lavinia Jordan, Janet Horsey.

Members of a Christmas pageant at Crowcombe organised by the Revd Peter Birkett, c.1960.

Beryl ('Nan') and Roly Ford, c.1944.

Jim Ford at Crowcombe, 1939.

Looking towards the Carew Arms in the late 1940s.

CROWCOMBE

The first articulated lorry cab purchased by Baker & Son, of Crowcombe Heathfield, 1983.

Northam Mill with a Singer car in the road, 1950s.

1st Crowcombe Boy Scouts, 1945.

William Baker, postman and saddler at Crowcombe in the late 1920s.

Left: Stanley Powe after feeding his pigs in the 1960s.

Annie Bailey with her cart-horse. Annie worked at the Crowcombe estate for 63 years.

William and Annie Herniman in their garden at Sunnyside (now Sunnybank), Crowcombe, in the 1930s.

Phyllis Bailey (later Mrs Herbert Herniman) astride a white cart-horse.

William and Annie Herniman. William was postman at Crowcombe for 43 years.

Phyllis Bailey (later Mrs Herbert Herniman) with Peggy the cow.

Fancy dress at Crowcombe, c.1970. Left to right: Diane Jenkins, Susan Herniman, Susan Jenkins.

CROWCOMBE

Harry Bale (sitting) and Ted Hunt working on the Crowcombe estate, c.1930s.

Jubilee tableaux in the Church House, 1935.

Helpers at a Crowcombe Church fête in the 1960s. Left to right: Dr Heineman, Mrs Cavill, Revd Peter Birkett, Phyllis Powe.

Borough Cottage, Crowcombe, celebrating a royal occasion.

Street scene at Crowcombe in Edwardian times.

The Blue Ball Inn (on right), *Triscombe, c.1920s.*

Triscombe Stone, c.1905. This Bronze Age, well-worn standing stone is a great antiquity and is reputed to have mysterious powers which will grant a wish to those who sit on it!

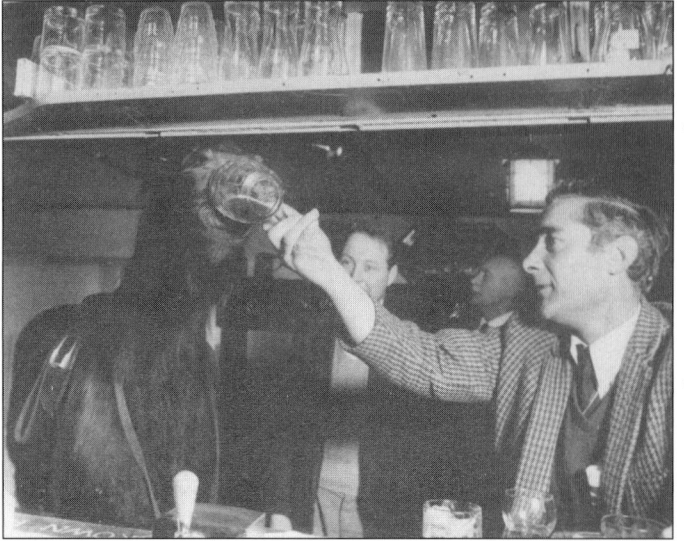

Jock the horse enjoying his daily pint of beer from his own glass held by John Hicks at the Blue Ball Inn, Triscombe, in the late 1960s. Also pictured are: David Parsons and Frank Mortimore. Jock could count his age by pawing the ground with a foot and lived until he was 44. Jock's drinking habit reached the ears of the BBC, who sent a TV crew to Triscombe to film him sampling his favourite tipple. However, Jock was camera shy and would not co-operate, promptly departing from the bar. The camera crew waited for a while but to no avail, so packed up and left. Ten minutes later in walked Jock to quietly enjoy his usual pint!

Meet of the Devon and Somerset Staghounds at Crowcombe Park Gate, 1907.

Triple Hunt meet on the Quantocks: the Devon and Somerset Staghounds, Quantock Staghounds and Tiverton Staghounds, c.1990. Left to right: Mrs Diane Scott, Walter Perry, ?, Maurice Scott, Roly Ford.

Roly Ford, Joint Master of the Quantock Staghounds, 1985–91.

Quantock Staghounds' chairman Nick Gibbons (left) and Joint Masters Enid Baker and Brian Palmer at the last meet at Crowcombe Park Gate before the Parliamentary ban on hunting with dogs came into force during February 2005.

Joint Masters Major and Mrs T.F. Trollope-Bellew at a meet of the Crowcombe Beagles at Capton in 1952.

Pheasant shoot at Triscombe in the 1930s.

Crowcombe Court

Crowcombe Court, c.1863.

The Quantock Hills has nestling under its wooded western slopes a magnificent Grade I listed early-Georgian mansion. Building started around 1723, using red brick with yellow Bath stone dressing in the English baroque style. Crowcombe Court was described by Nikolaus Pevsner in his book *The Buildings of England* as 'the finest house of its date in Somerset south of the Bath area'.

The present-day Crowcombe Court is the second house built in this location. In 1236 that half of Crowcombe, later known as the manor of Crowcombe Biccombe or Crowcombe Carew, was owned by Simon de Crowcombe. Crowcombe Studley was the name of the other manor of Crowcombe. The first manor-house was mentioned as far back as 1295, built north or west of the church, and by the mid-fourteenth century it included dovecots and a fishpond. Simon, grandson of Simon de Crowcombe, died without issue in 1349 and it passed to his niece Iseult, who by 1353 had married John Biccombe. It remained with the Biccombe family mainly through the female line until Hugh Biccombe died in 1568, leaving Crowcombe Biccombe to his daughter Elizabeth, wife of Thomas Carew, of Camerton, once suspected of complicity in the Babington Plot. Sir John Carew succeeded and was licensed to create a park and warren in 1616. Another John Carew laid out a court and gardens in 1676. John and Thomas were obviously popular forenames with the Carew family, as many descendants bore them.

One such Thomas inherited the old manor-house and huge estate at the age of 17 in 1719, but had to wait until he was 21 before having any authority over it. Between 1723 and 1734 Thomas, who was later a Member of Parliament for Minehead (1739–47), demolished the old manor-house and engaged builder/architect Thomas Parker, of Gittisham, Devon, to build the present-day mansion on a new site approximately 250 metres further up the slope from the old house with a long, straight drive leading to the village. This choice of architect was perhaps unfortunate because during demolition of the old house in 1724 Parker discovered bags of silver and silver coins hidden behind panelling in the hall and kept them. It is reputed that the money (one coin said to date 1662) and silver was hidden during the Monmouth Rebellion.

The north and south service and stable wings on the west side of the new house were built first, using material from the old house. The date on the weathervane shows the stable block was covered in 1725 and the initials on the vane are those of Thomas and his wife Mary Drewe, of Grange, Devon, whom he married shortly before undertaking the building project.

The foundations and basement of the main house were started around the time the service blocks were being completed, the entire storey being clad in stone with stone mullioned windows. It appears Parker was responsible for the vaulted engineering of this structure, including the network of channels which supplied fresh spring water to the house and drainage away to irrigate the walled garden. At the time of writing, these springs from an underground reservoir still supply water to the farm and to 50 houses in the village (Crowcombe Court has been on mains water since the 1960s/'70s). The water never sees the light of day until it comes out of the tap. The source of the water is said to be in Wales and the spring in the back lawn was once reputed to rise and fall with the tide! In 1732 payments to Parker ceased because of inaccurate accounts, double charging and failure to submit vouchers. In 1735 Parker's accomplice in the theft, James Gayland, a plumber, thinking he was dying, confessed to the Carews and a treasure trove court established the money Thomas Parker found hidden back in 1724 was rightfully Thomas Carew's. Parker was ruined; he was forced to hand over the land purchased with his ill-gotten gains and later was imprisoned in the Fleet for debt and apparently died there.

In 1734 Carew engaged Nathaniel Ireson, of Wincanton, as architect/builder to complete the house on the foundations already laid by Thomas Parker. The quarries at Lawford and Townsend Lane provided stone and lime for the building of

The stable yard at Crowcombe Court, c.1863.

Crowcombe Court, and the bricks used were made in the parish, either on site or in the brickfield at the southern end of the village, by John and Richard Newick, who used furze cut at Crowcombe Heathfield to fire the kilns. The kilns were thatched with reed and bricks surplus to Thomas Carew's needs were sold. He also allowed the rector clay to make bricks and gave him a kiln to rebuild part of the parsonage house in 1733.

The whole house cost Thomas Carew approximately £6,000 and to raise the money he had to sell six manors. It is also alleged 500 oak trees were felled in Watermans Wood for use in the building. The bark from the trees was offered for sale to tanners. The original bills, etc., for the building of Crowcombe Court, as it became known in 1741, are in the Somerset Record Office at Taunton, right down to the payment for the collection of faggots to light the brick kilns. Thomas also had laid out ornamental and kitchen gardens to the south of the house, extended the park and planted woods on the hill to the east. Thomas died in 1766 and was survived by two daughters, Mary (d.1774) and Elizabeth, who was the wife of James Bernard of the Middle Temple.

James Bernard built a hothouse and removed the ornamental gardens for a more naturalistic style. He also set out walks in the park and combe, a succession of weirs across the stream and a rustic bridge dated 1776. In the park behind the house, high above the stream about halfway up a steep wooded slope, is a cruciform 'ruin'. Constructed c.1776 and reputed to consist of fragments of a medieval building which came from Halsway Manor, it is known as Cardinal Beaufort's Chapel. Authentic Gothic mouldings appear in the folly, but a landscape picture of an earlier date seems to indicate an 'object' behind the present house exactly where this ruin stands. In the late-eighteenth century an icehouse was constructed in a steep bank above the stream. It was brick-built, shaped like an igloo and covered with earth with a 5-foot high wooden door.

Ruins of the Beaufort Chapel in Crowcombe Park.

The Honourable Mrs Ethel Mary Trollope.

Elizabeth and James Bernard were succeeded in 1811 by Mary, daughter of Elizabeth's first cousin, John Carew, of Anthony, in Cornwall. Mary married George Warrington, who took the additional name of Carew, as did his son, grandson and great-grandson, E.G. Carew, who died childless in 1886. The estate then passed to his sister Ethel Mary, wife of the Honourable Robert Cranmer Trollope, second son of Lord Kesteven, who purchased part of the Crowcombe Studley half of the manor in 1894, thus reuniting almost the two halves of Crowcombe. The Honourable Mrs Trollope died in 1934 and was succeeded in turn by her grandson, Anthony F. Trollope-Bellew, who died on active service in 1942, and upon his brother's death, by Major Thomas F. Trollope-Bellew. They were the sons of the Honourable Mrs Trollope's daughter, Nesta, who was a trustee of the estate and took up residence at the Court whenever she visited Somerset. She had married Colonel Bellew, of Okehampton Manor, Wiveliscombe, who in turn changed his name to Trollope-Bellew.

Over the years the entrance steps have been changed at least three times and the ground floor sash windows were altered from their Georgian style of London glass to windows of two panes as seen today.

The old bridge in Crowcombe Park, built in 1776.

CROWCOMBE

The entrance hall at Crowcombe Court, c.1863.

The interior of the Court had the appearance of a fashionable Bath house with much fine plaster decoration. The normal layout of an early-Georgian house was followed with a large hall in the neo-Palladian 'stone hall' style with rich stuccoed decoration. In 1739, six tons of Ketton stone were used in the hall, probably for the white stone flooring. Passing through the Serlian arch with its *verde antico* columns (painted to resemble marble), but now tragically almost destroyed by the use of modern paint, are the great stairs. The staircase of three flights, which rises only to the first floor, is in mahogany with twisted newels, carved cut strings and ramped handrail with a Serlian marbled columned window. Unfortunately, a short length of newels on the half-landing was probably destroyed by fire in 1963 and replaced by straight turned oak newels rather than the original twisted ones and ramped handrail. The fine stucco mouldings and ceiling centrepiece designed by Nathaniel Ireson featuring the Carew arms, one of the Court's finest focal points, was also lost in the fire when firemen broke through the ceiling from the gallery above in an attempt to control the blaze and save the house. The wall was adorned with pediment niches flanked by elaborate compositions verging on the rococo side of baroque.

The Carew coat of arms.

To the right of the hall was the great parlour with withdrawing-room, now known as the drawing-room, again with beautiful stucco mouldings. It is uncertain how much is the original. It is reputed to have been replanned and redecorated in the 1870s by Edward Barry. The frieze and door handles have the entwined initials GMC which are probably those of George Warrington Carew, who succeeded to the estate in 1855 and died in 1874, and his wife (Philippa) Mary. A set of plates with the initials PMGWC were reputed to have been a wedding present.

To the left of the hall is the dining-room with its unusual floor, on which a carpet-like design was painted or stencilled, centred on another representation of the family coat of arms. During the nineteenth century it was not uncommon for floors to be marbled or decorated in this style in place of carpets but, because of their vulnerability, painted floors rarely survived.

During the Second World War part of Crowcombe Court was home to a searchlight battalion who manned searchlights at the top of the combe, above Halsway and on Elworthy Burrows on the Brendons. Each site was equipped with a searchlight, Nissen hut for sleeping in, machine-gun and, of course, an

Colonel G.H. Warrington Carew's Harriers at Crowcombe Court, 1864–65. Left to right, back row: Mrs Carew with Edmund, Mrs Charlotte Mynors with Alice, Mrs Coventry Carew; front: J. Vicary, R. Chappell (on foot, kennelman), Colonel G.H. Warrington Carew, Mr Coventry Carew, ? Newton.

The indoor staff at Crowcombe Court, c.1863. Left to right, back row: Elizabeth, Samuel, Clara, ? Rowe; front: the cook, John, Sarah, Jane, Mr Gaye (butler), Mrs Wilkins, J. Vicary, Emily.

The outside staff at Crowcombe Court, 1863. Left to right, back row: Joseph Duddridge and ? Jordan (carpenters), ? Gaye (steward and butler), ?, ? Smainney; middle: ?, ?, John Barker, ? Jordan, ? Perriam, ? Gadd; front: ? Davis (cowman), G. Herniman, R. Chappell.

Thomas Carew, who built the present Crowcombe Court.

Crowcombe Court, 2004. Note the alterations to the entrance and ground-floor windows.

Elsan (toilet). One night the team on duty above Crowcombe caught an enemy plane in the searchlight's beam and fired at it. Naturally the gunner in the plane fired back, putting three holes in the Elsan – fortunately it was not in use at the time!

Major and Mrs Thomas Trollope-Bellew came to Crowcombe Court after their marriage in 1951, but after three years moved to Beadons, a smaller house in the village. In 1955 the Court became a residential home for the elderly, but in 1963 it suffered extensive damage from fire and from the vast quantities of water used to extinguish the blaze.

The Court was sold in 1968 and used for storage purposes with various rooms rented out. The house was rented by Brympton School, an independent boys' boarding-school, in 1974, but because of the cost of new building regulations it was forced to close in 1976. The Court was then sold again, but its condition proved difficult to maintain; the kitchen and stable wings were sold off separately and converted into apartments. In the 1980s the main house roof was replaced with new leads and was turned into a nursing home – which closed in 1999.

Crowcombe Court was sold again and is now undergoing the process of restoration. Once more the Court's principal rooms see happy family celebrations in the guise of weddings, receptions or other special occasions. Organisations also use them to entertain guests to lunches and dinners. So, perhaps, Crowcombe Court's fortunes have come almost full circle.

The Major

Crowcombe and more distant parts of the country, especially in the field of hunting and hounds, lost a large and colourful character when Major Thomas Fleming Trollope-Bellew, TD, died at his home at Crowcombe in March 1993, aged 72. The eldest son of Colonel and the Honourable Mrs Trollope-Bellew, of Casewick, near Stamford, Lincolnshire, he was born at the family house in London, but was brought up at the beautiful family property of Casewick. It was here that he started to acquire his profound knowledge of wildlife and natural history that was to stand him in good stead thereafter.

Educated at Radley, he did not take up his place at Sidney Sussex College, Cambridge, because of the outbreak of the Second World War. Instead he proudly served with the 6th Battalion Royal Lincolnshire Regiment in France until 1940 when he was evacuated with his men, complete with weapons and equipment, from Dunkirk. He later contributed to the defence of the South Coast during the Battle of Britain, on attach-

At the last meet of the Crowcombe Beagles, 1985. Left to right: Daphne, Anthony H., Martin and Major Thomas F. Trollope-Bellew.

ment to the Buffs, after which in 1941 he was posted to the Punjab, attached to the Indian Army.

When he returned to England in 1946 he went home to Lincolnshire, where he formed the Casewick Bassett Hounds and Casewick Cricket Club. After serving for some years on Kesteven County Council, he married Daphne Wainwright, daughter of a housemaster at Stamford School. Following their marriage in 1951 they set up home at Crowcombe Court. He had inherited the Crowcombe estate from his grandmother, the Honourable Mrs Ethel Mary Trollope, following the death of his brother Anthony in action at El Alamein in 1942. Anthony was the second heir to the Crowcombe estate to lose his life during war as the third Lord Kesteven had died of his wounds during the First World War. The Major's grandfather was distantly related to the fox-hunting Victorian novelist Anthony Trollope.

The Major brought his pack of Bassett hounds with him to Crowcombe, hunting them until 1965. He resumed his interest in 1971 when he established the Crowcombe Beagles, retaining the Hunt button of his ancestor, Colonel George Henry Warrington Carew, who had founded the Crowcombe Harriers and built the kennels. For many years he wrote the hunting reports for the Quantock Staghounds, and was chairman of the West Somerset Foxhounds for nine years.

His role in local government saw him serve on the former Williton Rural District Council, including a term as chairman, and he was elected to Somerset County Council in 1973, remaining a councillor until 1985. He also had the distinction of serving as chairman of the Exmoor National Park Authority for four years from 1974.

The Major was a very precise man and everything was done by the book, but he also had a softer side, being of an extremely kind and hospitable disposition. He quietly did many people favours, always

Major Thomas F. Trollope-Bellew.

with a minimum of fuss. As well as his great love of hunting, he also had an enduring passion for cricket, being president of Crowcombe Cricket Club at the time of his death. He could often be seen attired in an umpire's white coat.

In 1954 the Major and his wife moved to Beadons in the village and in 1955 Crowcombe Court became a residential home for the elderly. In 1965 they moved to The Cottage (now known as Hooks) and in 1983 moved into The Bungalow, which the Major had built. This was where he died.

The Church of the Holy Ghost at Crowcombe was packed to overflowing with people from all walks of life, not just locally but nationally as well, for the Major's funeral. It was conducted by the Revd Malcolm Bole, assisted by four priests. Complying with the Major's wishes, prior to the service there was a medley consisting of 'The Lincolnshire Poacher', 'John Peel', 'Men of Harlech' and 'All Through the Night'; 'Land of Hope and Glory' was the voluntary. During the playing of the final hymn the coffin was carried from the church, preceded by a procession made up of the chairman and clerk of the Parish Council, churchwardens, hunt servants in livery, agents and tenants of the Crowcombe, Barholm (Lincolnshire) and Carew Castle (Pembrokeshire) estates, members of Crowcombe Cricket Club in whites, employees and the clergy. The Major's grave was lined with gorse and 'Gone Away' was blown by Richard Down, huntsman of the Quantock Staghounds.

The Major's eldest son Anthony is now lord of the manor and runs the Crowcombe estate. He and his wife Annabel and daughters Emma and Harriet reside at Hurley Farm, which he farms. Martin, the Major's younger son, runs the Lincolnshire estate.

Ruth Tongue: Folklorist, Author, Eccentric

One of the characters of Crowcombe was Ruth Lyndall Tongue, niece of composer Sir Edward German. She was born in 1898 at Handworth, near Birmingham, where her father, Edwin Tongue, was a Congregational minister. Miss Tongue had two brothers, and when she was aged two the family moved to Taunton where her father was minister at a chapel in North Street. The Tongue family left Taunton in 1909 to reside at Harrow, Middlesex. She was educated at Bishop Fox's School, Taunton, Harrow High School, Harrow School of Art, and the London College of Music. Miss Tongue claimed to be a chime child – that is, she was born after midnight on a Friday and before cock-crow on a Saturday. This gave her a certain

Wharncliffe, a former home of Ruth Tongue, which was destroyed by fire, c.1960.

magic aura in the eyes of some people, and she did indeed go on to prove to be a 'gifted' child. Like many old Somerset beliefs, this had died out by the First World War.

She had been a prolific collector of folk material since childhood, and among the books she wrote on the subject were *The Chime Child or Somerset Singers*, *Somerset Folklore* and a slim volume of *Four Quantock Carols*. Her last book was *The Forgotten Folk-Tales of the English Counties*, which is almost a roll-call of the great names of English popular narrative. She was without doubt a genius of folklore.

In 1954 Miss Tongue came to Crowcombe, where she joined the Women's Institute and wrote, produced and appeared in plays which members performed in the Church House. She was involved in a folk-music centre at Halsway Manor in the 1960s and also ran a children's folk theatre. One of her local homes in the woods above Crowcombe Court was at Wharncliffe, which was largely destroyed by fire in 1966 when many of her folklore manuscripts were lost.

A great country and animal lover, Miss Tongue was co-founder with Leslie Pike of the local Mountain and Moorland Pony Show, which was first held at The Rookery and later at Crowcombe Court by permission of Major T.F. Trollope-Bellew. The Revd Peter Birkett was the announcer for the original show and recalled Miss Tongue's eccentric appearance, driving her trotter Miranda, sitting aloft in a bowler hat, a satin blouse and very baggy jodhpurs. She was prominent in the running of the Pony Show for about 18 years in an easy-going, laid-back manner, much to the enjoyment of the children, with whom she had an excellent repartee. She started the Cub Scouts at Crowcombe Court and was also good at handling difficult boys, getting the best out of them by being patient and helping them to be responsible.

Ruth Tongue.

Almost as much a character as herself was Miss Tongue's donkey, Selina Mouse II. The donkey lived to a great age and Miss Tongue would have her indoors on a cold winter's night, where she would lie in front of the fire.

As well as at Wharncliffe, Miss Tongue resided at a cottage at Roebuck. She kept ponies at The Rookery (now demolished), which she rented from Mrs Lewis. The tack and harness were stored in the deserted cottage. In her latter years she suffered from failing eyesight and crippling arthritis, spending much time in a wheelchair. She died at Williton Hospital in September 1981.

Tony Horsey: Distinguished Service and Flying Career

Member of a well-known local family who came from Stogumber to reside at Crowcombe for many years, B.A. (Tony) Horsey decided on a career in the Armed Forces. Born in 1933, Tony first attended Stogumber School and then moved on to Williton School at the age of 11. Leaving school at the age of 14, Tony first worked as an apprentice garage mechanic and a farm labourer until joining the Army as a boy soldier in the Royal Artillery in 1950.

In 1955 Tony was selected for pilot training at Royal Air Force, Middle Wallop, being awarded his wings in 1956. During 1956–59 he flew on reconnaissance and target marking sorties against the Chinese Communists in Malaya, flying for approximately 3,000 hours on active service operations on fixed-wing aircraft. During this period Tony was awarded the Distinguished Flying Medal and was mentioned in Despatches. He was presented with his medal by HM the Queen at Buckingham Palace in 1959.

During subsequent years Tony flew fixed wing and helicopters on active service in Borneo and also did flying tours in Germany, Thailand and the USA (attached for helicopter training to the US Army). His short tour in Thailand was for daily reconnaissance sorties along the Mekong River to the Cambodian border during the Vietnam War. In 1968 he attended the Central Flying School RAF on an instructor's course, subsequently going on instructional tours as chief flying instructor in the Far East and Europe. Then in 1973 Tony became officer commanding the Gazelle Training Fleet, responsible for training flying instructors and the introduction of the Gazelle helicopter into the Army operational role.

In 1975 Tony resigned his commission as captain and took an appointment as company test pilot with Westland Helicopters at Yeovil, moving to Combe St Nicholas with his wife Mary and sons David, Robert and Dan. He obtained his airline transport pilot's licence (UK Civil Aviation Authority) and Ministry of Defence (Procurement) production, research and development test pilot approval for Sea King, Commando, Lynx, Gazelle, Scout and Wasp helicopters.

Captain B.A. (Tony) Horsey, DFM.

Tony took a change of scenery in 1977 when he was appointed officer commanding a training squadron and chief flying instructor of the Qatar Emiri Air Force (in the Gulf, next to Saudi Arabia). Westland built all the military helicopters for use there and Tony was asked to take a uniformed appointment as a major and set up a training squadron. He did not remain in this position long, for in 1978 he joined the Royal Flight of Oman to fly Pumas and Super Pumas and was also training captain. Tony was then appointed as a personal pilot to Sultan Qaboos, the ruler of the Sultanate of Oman, who was educated in the UK and went to Sandhurst. In 1987 Tony was awarded the Royal Order of the Emblem of Oman and the Royal Guard Medal.

For medical reasons Tony retired from flying in 1988 and took an appointment as conservator of stained glass at Canterbury Cathedral. He retired in 1998 and now lives with his wife in Kent.

Tony Horsey after receiving the Royal Order of the Emblem of Oman from Sultan Qaboos, 1987.

A Crowcombe Childhood

The authors are grateful to Mary Rhodes (also known as Bridget Jordan) for the following reflections on her childhood days at Crowcombe:

One of the most remarkable and incongruous events of my childhood in Crowcombe occurred when I was about eight. My sisters and I walked home from church one Sunday to find many shiny, large, alien-looking cars outside our house; indoors we were overrun by journalists – paparazzi – men in city suits, items almost never seen in the village during the 1950s. This sophisticated invasion was my first indication that not only was there an entirely different way of life somewhere out there beyond our boundaries, but that also it might be empowered to overlap with our own very restricted and protected existence. The furore concerned Peter Townsend and his relationship with Princess Margaret, about which I knew nothing at all. It was not considered a fit subject for young ears, but the Old Forge, in which the Townsends had lived for some years, had been our property, later sold.

As children we led a tranquil and secure existence, knowing that it was the natural and only place where we could live. Our great-grandfather, Charles Jordan, had built our house and shop; gravestones in the churchyard marked the family back to our four-time great-grandparents, born in the 1750s, and members of the family were paying taxes in the village in 1641 – there was no other place so appropriate. My mother, however, was slightly less convinced, having been born in Cardiff and studied in London she needed to adjust somewhat to the culture of Crowcombe, where she initially arrived as district nurse. There was no electricity in the village until the early 1950s (I remember watching it being installed). Television crept in slowly; the hills interfered with the signal, causing some restrictions. Dr Meyers from Stogumber held a surgery at Miss Baker's house on Tuesday and Thursday afternoons. Buses went through the village every two hours to Taunton and Minehead. When I went to school in Taunton from the age of 10 I had to cycle to and from Crowcombe station daily to go in on the train, with quite a walk at the Taunton end!

We naturally knew everybody in the village and where they lived. We played in the middle of the road during the hopscotch season (using Watchet alabaster as chalk), for cars were few and far between. We did a great deal of walking, particularly when we were small – down the village to school, in a crocodile to the Church House for school dinners, to church and back every Sunday morning, then on Sunday afternoons our father would take us out for a walk, sometimes round Heddon Oak and Lawford or Slough, but more frequently over the hills, up through Burgage, then either bearing right to Crowcombe Park Gate and down the combe or Little Quantock or bearing left to come down through Halsway Quarry and back along the main road. I don't know if my father had an agenda for these long and varied walks, but it certainly ensured that we came to know our area very well indeed.

Until I was seven we lived in the middle of the three Hagleys cottages (compulsorily purchased in 1963 to make way for Hagleys Green). After the death of my grandmother, Edith Jordan, we moved into Hagleys House, the premises of the village shop. We enjoyed the freedom of a good-sized orchard where we kept hens, and there were many outhouses to play in. We also had a meadow where Mr Cyril Lock kept his cows – the rent for the meadow was paid as skimmed milk and cream at weekends, an excellent business arrangement.

Mary Rhodes.

The rural isolation of the village could have meant that our lives lacked stimulation, but it was autonomous and worked well as a community. We had a selection of strong-minded leaders who ensured that, for children at any rate, there was never a lack of things to do.

The rector (the Revd Peter Birkett) was one of the principals in this respect. He was lively, enthusiastic and innovative. He loved theatricals; he was forever inventing and creating new village entertainments involving both children and adults. He held a coster market in the stable yard. There was a cycle of mystery plays produced and acted in the church in conjunction with Mr St John Couch from Bicknoller. Every winter the rector developed a new form of Christmas entertainment, and the children were always taken carol singing, usually piled into Land Rovers to various farms and outposts of the parish. One memorable year we were dressed up for a Nativity pageant on a farm trailer and pulled through the village by tractor. The head of the village school at the time was Mrs Winifred Reynish; she encouraged and supported us in these activities.

It seems that we were forever dressing up! During these years we were simultaneously involved in folk theatre, gymkhanas and other recreated 'traditional' pastimes organised by Ruth Tongue, who then lived at Wharncliffe Cottage. Theatre and animals were her passions and she did her best to propagate them; she also collected folklore, mainly through lecturing at local Women's Institutes. She kept her ponies at The Rookery in Lawford, teaching many of us to ride, whereupon we were trundled round to all the local gymkhanas and pony club events – more dressing up!

Major T.F. Trollope-Bellew was another personality – perhaps more because of his actual existence rather than through any activities he required of us. Every house belonging to the estate had its doors and window frames painted a standard blue, thus enabling everyone to identify his properties; much of the parkland was out of bounds.

My mother, Winifred Jordan, initiated a junior branch of the St John Ambulance Cadets at Crowcombe; this was affiliated to the division which she ran at Bishops Lydeard.

The really important regular events at Crowcombe were cricket and the Hunt. My father was seriously involved with the cricket; in the 1950s he no longer played, but he was an umpire, and had been secretary *during his playing years. The team was disbanded for a while, but summer Saturday afternoons were given over to cricket, both when I was a small child and later during my teens.*

Two other strong memories for me are of the Coronation celebrations in 1953 (more fancy dress!) where we watched the giant caterpillar processing through the street, and of the snow in the winter of 1962–63. The snow began on the day after Boxing Day, and we were more or less cut off until mid-March. As I was taking my O levels that year I was not permitted to miss many weeks at school and had to be billeted out; it gave me great kudos among my school friends.

Childhood in Crowcombe was an adventure, it was mostly good; it was not easy but we knew no alternative. My own memories are obviously totally subjective, but it was above all for me constant, safe and secure.

Crowcombe Cricket Club

In 1993 Crowcombe Cricket Club celebrated its centenary and to help mark the occasion the then local MP, Tom King, brought a strong team to the village to play against the local side. During the tea interval Mr King unveiled a plaque on a new scorebox presented to the club by Mrs Daphne Trollope-Bellew in memory of her late husband, Major Thomas F. Trollope-Bellew, who had died earlier that year. He was president of the club for 32 years and was keenly interested in the game. Mr King was presented with a Crowcombe centenary cricket cap.

In its beautiful setting under the Quantocks, at the time of writing the ground is kept in excellent condition by cricket groundsman Joe Bailey, who produces excellent playing strips from experience gained from playing for Crowcombe since 1957 and captaining the side for 20 years. The club also has the benefit of an all-weather playing pitch.

Among cricketers who have served the club well over the years are Jack Barber, Cyril Lock, George Webber, Brian ('Tich') Baker, Graham Hunt, Joe Bailey, Chris Brewer and members of the Lewis and Rexworthy families. The club was featured in *The Times* in 1996 when a writer waxed lyrical on the sumptuous cricket teas provided at Crowcombe.

The club runs First, Second and Sunday XIs at present and has enjoyed considerable playing success in recent years. In 2003 the First XI was West Somerset League Division I champions and winners of the West Somerset League Knockout Cup, with Paul Bradbury being First XI player of the year. Another successful season followed in 2004 with the First XI being Division I runners-up to arch-rivals Stogumber, the title being decided in the last league match. Chris Brewer, who first played for Crowcombe in 1975, was First XI player of the year in 2004.

A splendid addition to the facilities of the club and the village is the new Crowcombe Hall, which was opened in 2003 on the site of the old cricket pavilion. It includes a wide range of sport and leisure facilities with excellent changing rooms, showers and toilets.

Major T.F. Trollope-Bellew with oldest son Anthony, c.1970.

Groundsman Joe Bailey, 2004.

All-rounder Chris Brewer, 2004.

John Baker (captain), 2004.

Fast bowler Chris Lewis, 2004.

Crowcombe cricket team, 1928. Left to right, back row: Charlie Grant, ?, Frank Salter, Jim Harris, F. Westcott, Jim Hall, Edward Merson, ?, Jack Spencer, ? MacDonald; middle: George Merson, Jack Barber, Fred Smith, Jack Hayes, Ern Hayes, Cyril Lock, Reg Jennings, Bert Durrant; front: Geoff Routley.

Crowcombe cricket team, 1933. Left to right, back row: L. Goodrich, E. Griffiths, Jim Merson, Bill Payne, Alf Clarke, Frank Board, David Salter, Frank Salter, Jim Griffiths; seated: Geoff Routley, George Merson, Cyril Lock, Edward Merson, Revd H. Christian Young, Jack Barber (captain), Les Jordan, Tom Jewell, Albert Welsher; front: Ken Webber (scorer).

Crowcombe Cricket Club, 1982. Left to right, back row: D. Shattock (scorer), J. Dyer, R. Lewis, T. Ash, P. Ash, R. Rexworthy, M. Baker; front: J. Bailey (S. Bailey sitting), P. Rexworthy, C. Brewer (captain), G. Hunt, A. Godfrey.

Crowcombe Cricket Club centenary team, 1993. Left to right, back row: Mr George Dent (chairman), Richard Lewis (umpire), Peter Rexworthy, Chris Brewer, Martin Baker, Steve Hole, Mark Blake, Tyrone Ash, Mr V. Brewer (vice-chairman); front: Stuart Bailey, Rob Phillips, Joe Bailey (captain), Robert Bushrod, James Rexworthy; on ground: Robbie Rexworthy (scorer).

Crowcombe Cricket Club, West Somerset League Knockout Cup winners, 1994. Left to right, back row: P. Rexworthy, M. Baker, T. Ash, S. Hole, I. Rew, S. Perry; front: C. Lock, S. Bailey, C. Brewer, J. Rexworthy, R. Phillips.

Crowcombe 1st XI, 2004. West Somerset League Division I champions and winners of the West Somerset League Knockout Cup, 2003. Left to right, back row: Peter Warne, Chris Lewis, Nick Nation, Tyrone Ash, Tom Baker, Chris Brewer, Mr Richard Boddington (chairman), Martin Baker, Joe Bailey (umpire); front: Chris Lock, Jacob Smith, John Baker (captain), Stuart Bailey.

Coronation Celebrations, 1953

Mounted tableaux and costumed children brought humour and colour into Queen Elizabeth II's Coronation Day festivities at Crowcombe on Tuesday 2 June 1953. Unfortunately rain curtailed sports and some other events that were to have taken place in Broad Meadow. The organising committee had Major T.F. Trollope-Bellew as its chairman and Mr A. Biss as secretary, and Mrs Kelland was convenor of a tea committee.

In the morning the rector, the Revd P. Birkett, conducted a service in the Church of the Holy Ghost, and the celebrations began in the afternoon with a tableaux and costume assembly by Broad Meadow. Entries were judged by Dr Heineman and Mrs Hill (Quarkhill). They awarded first prize to a tableau entry by Crowcombe Court employees and their children depicting the first Queen Elizabeth and a retinue. This was a most fascinating turn out, to which an ancient brougham (a horse-drawn closed carriage) borrowed from the Court lent quite an air. Those taking part (and they were in striking costumes) were the Misses Janet Scott (queen), Rosemary Gibbs, Dorothy Colman and Janet Labbe, and Messrs Harry Bale (coachman), L. Gadd, Somerfield, E. Colman, M. Gibbs and C. Chiplin.

Second prize was awarded to an ingenious entry by the Guild of Church Workers styled 'The Gurt Wurm' and it earned many plaudits on the score of humour and originality. Those forming the 'gurt wurm' were Mrs S. Powe, Mrs Birkett, Mr W. Smith, Mr W.F. Chidley, Miss M. Bailey and Miss H. Chidley. Another Elizabethan tableau, entered by the Women's Institute, gained third prize, the characters being depicted by Mrs Strong (queen), Mrs Cooper, Mrs E. Welsher, Mr Chris Cooper, Mrs W. Cottrell and Mr L. Berryman.

Fancy-dress competitors at the Crowcombe Coronation celebrations for Queen Elizabeth II, 1953. Left to right: Agnes Pike, Ethel Routley, ?, Ethel Welsher.

There were classes for children on horseback, with escorts, and several pretty scenes were depicted. Prizewinners were: 1, St George and Old England (Tony Lewis and Judy, Bunty and Bruce Owens); 2, Maid Marian (Josie Owens with Mary Lewis, escort); 3, Richard of Taunton Deane (Edward and Ricky Lewis). Prizes for walking entries were won by: 1, C. Welsher (pirate); 2, Lavinia and Mary Jordan (Alice in Wonderland and the white rabbit); 3, Eileen and Michael Webber (rabbits).

There was a procession up the village street, parishioners joining in, and it ended on the green outside the church, where mugs were presented to the children by Mrs J.N. Slater. Mrs Kelland and her ladies had prepared an excellent tea in the Church House. Afterwards it was too wet to do very much in Broad Meadow, so the children were amused at the school where a puppet show was given.

The day ended with a dance in the Church House, to the music of Sid Bryant's Band.

One of the horse-drawn floats in the Crowcombe Coronation parade, 1953.

Painting in West Somerset

Renowned local artist Barry Watkin, FRSA, now resides in Crowcombe. His work is much sought after and, as well as private commissions, he has held many one-man shows in Somerset and has exhibited in London with the Royal Society of British Artists and the Pastel Society. Mr Watkin has kindly penned the following article on some aspects of his painting career:

Barry Watkin, FRSA.

In 1988 my wife and I sold our business in Surrey and bought a fifteenth-century farmhouse in Kingswood, near Stogumber. For 15 years we ran residential painting holidays in a part of Somerset that must rate as one of Nature's gems: Exmoor and the Quantocks. Over the years I have spent many rewarding days exploring these two magical areas armed with sketchbook, Ordnance Survey map and painting gear, and still I'm finding new corners.

Most of my work is in pastel, a medium I have specialised in for nearly 20 years. Although most of my early work as a landscape painter was in oils, pastel suited my style perfectly as I like to get on with it, finishing a painting in one or two sessions. The three paintings reproduced on these pages are all pastels.

There is an enormous range of subject matter in this locality, including hills, rivers, small harbours – Porlock Weir has it all – and coastal scenes such as Kilve, West Quantoxhead and Porlock Bay. The villages, too, have much to offer the artist, but getting the angle right is sometimes hazardous. I once set up my easel in the middle of the road in order to capture the wonderful play of light on the Notley Arms pub in Monksilver. A tractor and trailer suddenly appeared from a side turning and the farmer stopped in astonishment, advising me to move before I got knocked over. I did not and was not, thanks mainly to some fancy footwork! Bicknoller has a lovely corner near the church. My students liked it because they could always pop into the pub for a quick one between sessions. Just up from the church is a delightful thatched cottage and over the years I have painted it from different angles, in watercolour and pastel, but the biggest challenge came when I was commissioned to paint the village from the lower slopes of the Quantocks. Apparently the local shop needed postcards of the view to meet demand from visitors.

Crowcombe Park Gate, from an original painting by Barry Watkin.

CROWCOMBE

Bicknoller village framed by the Quantocks (Barry Watkin).

It became a major work requiring five sessions, and it was on one of them that John Lees, chairman of the local Parish Council, walked up to me saying that he had had a number of telephone calls from residents complaining that there was a man on the hillside looking into their bedroom windows. I quickly pointed out that the nearest house was at least a quarter of a mile away and if I had been able to see anything it would have been so small I doubted whether it could have had any effect on my blood pressure!

A few years later I was asked to produce a painting of Bicknoller village by a lady who wished to present it to the residents. It now hangs in the Village Hall. I opted for a south-westerly aspect with the Quantocks in the background. This set off the buildings, particularly the church, to great effect. The time of year plays a significant part in the success or otherwise of a painting and I chose early spring when the trees were only lightly dressed. This enabled me to pick out many of the individual cottages which might otherwise have been obscured in mid-summer.

Just outside Sampford Brett, on the eastern side of the village, is an archaeological gem – a rock face about 20 metres high, of red and yellow sandstone, which rises up from a plateau of grass and wild flowers. I stumbled on it late one August afternoon when the colours were glowing in the warm sunshine, complemented by the vivid greens of bushes and small trees growing out of, and on top of, the cliff face. It reminded me of the great Norwich painter John Sell Cotman's watercolour of The Devil's Elbow, Rokeby Park. In an hour and a half I completed a working sketch from which I was able to produce the pastel reproduced on these pages. Some months later I added a group of Freisian cows for a touch of life and interest.

I have to admit that the beech trees at the top of Crowcombe Park Gate have provided me with material for any number of paintings. The view looking up the hill is always a winner, particularly in autumn, but three years ago I tackled it from the reverse angle, looking downhill. The trees on the left were in shadow and created a wonderful contrast with those on the right which were ablaze with colours ranging from yellow through orange, russet and red. If anyone would like to see my work, my annual exhibition is held during the last few days of November in Crowcombe Hall.

Rock face near Sampford Brett (Barry Watkin).

Crowcombe School, c.1900.

Extracts from Crowcombe CE School Logbook, 1926–55

The following extracts make fascinating reading and reflect wider social changes. No names have been mentioned here where embarrassment might be caused, and only initials have been inserted in certain places. The logbook is kept at the Somerset Record Office, Taunton. The school opened in 1872, but no logbooks are available before 1926. Owing to the 50-year rule, we are unable to publish further extracts.

1926

Members of school staff: Edith M. Bennett, R.A. Pugh, D.M. Richards.

5 Feb: Average attendance this week 57. Number on roll 61.

People attending the ceremony of the laying of the foundation-stone for Crowcombe Church of England School, which was opened in 1872.

17 Feb: Ash Wednesday – children attended service in church.

16 March: Nurse Mills visited the school this afternoon and examined the children's heads.

26 March: Six children sat for the compulsory examination.

13 April: School reopened after Easter holiday. Sixty scholars present, 63 on books.

15 April: Older girls commenced cookery course at Williton.

6 May: Girls could not attend cookery centre today, train service being dislocated owing to General Strike. The Hon. Mrs Trollope visited the school today.

17 May: Dr Parker attended to examine a boy for traces of ringworm of the scalp.

7 June: The Rector distributed attendance prizes for the year given under the James and Carew charities. Alice Shattock of Class II made a full attendance – 416 times.

11 June: An outbreak of mumps has reduced the attendance to 47 this week.

17 Aug.: School reopened after a month's holiday. Only 53 scholars present out of 65.

3 Sept: Attendance improved considerably this week, the average being 63. Number on roll 69.

25 Oct: The following report has been received by the managers from the Board of Education: 'Attainments in the head teacher's class are generally creditable and in some subjects (e.g. drawing and nature study) distinctly above the average. The teaching of the juniors has improved considerably during the past year; composition is the best subject. The children recently promoted from the infants' division are somewhat backward. Their teacher has been experimenting with a method which has

CROWCOMBE

been found successful elsewhere; it seems desirable that she should have a short course of training. At the present time the chief need of the school seems to be for the head teacher, who is a skilful class teacher herself, to devise means of leaving her large and difficult class in order to advise the two supplementary teachers on points of detail. The managers are to be congratulated on enlarging the cloakroom.'

28 Oct: A thoroughly wet day – only 25 children present.

1927
26 Jan: The Rector brought three dozen new Prayer Books today for use in school.
31 March: Miss D.M. Richards resigned her post as assistant teacher. Average attendance for the year 57; average number on books 66.
26 April: School reopened after Easter holiday with 58 children present and 62 on the books. Miss Olive Edith Brooks commenced duty as uncertificated assistant teacher today.
18 May: Alexander McDonald has been successful in passing Part I of the county examination for free places in secondary schools.
24 May: The Hon. Mrs Trollope visited the school this morning and invited teachers and scholars to tea at Crowcombe Court in celebration of Empire Day.
16 Aug: School reopened today after summer holiday. Very wet morning so only 39 children present; 59 on books.
5 Sept: Nurse Mills inspected the schoolchildren this morning and expressed her pleasure at finding them so clean.
11 Nov: The 'Two Minutes Silence' was reverently observed in school this morning; the flag was hoisted.
19 Dec: Only 37 children present owing to severe weather and prevalence of colds.

1928
23 March: The number of children on books had fallen to 52.
11 June: A dental inspection was held at the Church House this morning; 26 children were treated by the dentist.
16 Aug: A half-day's holiday was granted by the managers this afternoon to allow the children to attend the local flower show and sports.
25 Oct: Today I resign my position as head teacher of the school – Edith M. Bennett.
30 Oct: I have today commenced my duties as temporary headmistress of this school – C.M. George.
21 Dec: I have today completed my duties at this school – C.M. George.

1929
7 Jan: Today the new headmistress commenced duties in the school – J.M.A. Jowetts.
15 Feb: Only 12 children came to school owing to the blizzard, of these five came by bus. School was therefore closed.
1 & 8 Nov: The following pupils took dairy tests: Sidney Rich, James Henson, Phyllis Baker, Vera Coles, Percy Fowkes, Peggy Hebditch, Mildred Jordan, Kenneth Webber, Ernest Bellamy, William Neyens. Note: This class has shown great keenness, but cannot think for itself! – I. Welch, dairy instructress.

1930
14 March: The following children took the scholarship examination: Mildred Jordan, Phyllis Baker, Olive Ames, James Savage, Kenneth Webber, Gordon Pickersgill, William Bellamy.
24 May: The children competed in the Quantock Area Athletic Sports at Watchet. Peggy Hebditch won first prize for high jump and James Henson came second in the 80 yards flat race under 12. Phyllis Baker came third in the thread the needle race.
27 Nov: Report by HM Inspector Mrs A.M. Moore: 'The headmistress has brought much enthusiasm to bear on the problems of this school. In the short period since her appointment she has vivified the instruction and established a higher standard of attainment... In her endeavours she has been well supported by her assistants...'

1931
2 July: Nine boys attend a woodwork class at Williton for the day.
27 Oct: School closed for the General Election.

1932
4 March: Ten children sat for the qualifying examination for free places: D. Kelland, E. Parsons, E. Warren, B. Harris, S. Bellamy, D. Crane, P. Baker, C. Bates, J. Henson, S. Neyens.
24 Oct: Dairy class held in Church House under instruction of Miss A.M. Evans. Practical work done at Mr Case's farm in the afternoon. Children attending: O. Ames, B. Chilcott, B. Harris, K. Rich, E. Warren, P. Baker, G. Clark, P. Fowkes, I. Harris, J. Henson, L. Gibbs, W. Stark.

1933
31 Jan: The junior mistress, Miss O.E. Brooks, resigned her post.
1 Feb: Miss Marshall began her duty as junior mistress.
8 Feb: Miss Marshall had to abandon work in the school on account of illness.
24 Feb: School closed owing to heavy snow.
13 March: Miss Wedlake took up duties with the junior school.
3 April: Miss Wedlake left.
20 May: Olive Duddridge and Vera Merson attend Minehead County School for Part II of the scholarship examination.
17 Oct: Nine boys did not attend woodwork class at Watchet today owing to the prevalence of scarlet fever.

1934
12–15 Feb: The stove in the infants' room would not burn

Crowcombe CE VA School Infants, c.1958. Among those pictured are: Roger Webber, Susan Jordan, Rita Smith, Lucy Pike, Wendy Adams, Jane Duddridge.

Crowcombe CE VA School Seniors, c.1958. Left to right, back row: John Routley, Edward Lewis, ?, Tony Higgs, Chris Chilcott; middle: Bruce Owen, Colin Norman, Alan Strong, Michael Webber, Richard Day, Keith Brown, Peter Culverwell; front: Barbara Brown, Linda Bishop, Gillian Rich, Shirley Powe, Diana Criddle, Janet Burley, Mary Jordan, Marion Fisher.

CROWCOMBE

Crowcombe CE VA School, late 1950s. Left to right, back row: *?, Elfreda Mackie, Angela Bishop, Diana Berryman, Linda Bishop, Susan Smith;* middle: *Margaret Neyens, Bridget Webber, Joan Norman, Eileen Webber, David Newcombe, Jenny Neyens, Janet Besley, Susan Routley, Jackie Higgs;* front: *Peter Thorne, Peter Woolway, Brian Pike, Paul Duddridge, Nigel Rich, ? Carter, Richard Criddle, Peter Lazare.*

Crowcombe CE VA School, c.1960. Left to right, back row: *Miss Bray, Gillian Rich, ?, Christopher Criddle, Denzil Harris, ?, Bill Neyens, Peter Rexworthy, Martin Mackie, Stephen and Helen Barnes, Barbara Chilcott, Mrs Reynish (head);* third row: *Peter Lazare, Christopher Norman, June Kingston, Lucy Pike, Susan Jordan, Caroline Farmer, Jean Chilcott, Heather Rich, Sylvia Rexworthy, Ann Betts, ?, ? Besley, Wendy Adams, Roger Webber, David Denman;* second row: *Christopher Lock, Christopher Rexworthy, Jenny Webber, Geraldine Lock, Alison Marks, Jane Duddridge, Mary Hunt, Barbara Rexworthy, Charles Chilcott, Andrew Henson;* front: *? Norman, Charles Lewis, Paul Duddridge, Brian Gibbs, Nicholas Mackie.*

24 July:	*and the room constantly filled with smoke – chimney sweep sent for.*
	A girl so upset the discipline of the school that it was necessary to send her out.
28 Sept:	*D. Gadd, I. Bellamy and D. Crane have fallen in playground during physical training exercises and have badly cut their knees.*
5 Nov:	*Dairy classes held for week. Practical work in afternoon for following senior children: Bessie Harris, Eileen Warren, Glenys Conibeare, Lucy Denbury, Sylvia Bickham, Percy Baker, L. Neyens, E. Parsons, H. Herniman, J. Henson.*

1935

28 Feb:	*D.S. and her brother have scarlet fever and have been removed to the Isolation Hospital.*

1936

7 Jan:	*Miss R.A. Lockyer has left on account of the reduction in numbers on books – 47.*
14 Sept:	*Head teacher M. Jowett returned to duty.*

1937

18 Jan:	*School closed owing to floods.*
29 Jan:	*School closed owing to village being snowbound.*
5 March:	*Five children sat scholarship examination: Ivy Beavis, E. Jewell, W. Bale, Percy Crane and B. Stark. The Revd H. Christian Young invigilated.*
10 March:	*Snow – only 11 children attended, school closed for day.*
22 March:	*A blizzard set in at 11a.m. All children sent home, school closed at 2.15.*
12 May:	*School closed for Coronation Day and Whitsuntide holiday.*
6 July:	*Cookery classes begin in Bishops Lydeard. Six girls (B. Dunant, E. Jewell, I. Beavis, I. Walford, R. Conibeare and June Bellamy) attended, Mr C. Lock taking them by car.*
8 Dec:	*Only 20 children attended school.*

1938

17 Nov:	*School closed for by-election for Bridgwater constituency.*
28 Nov:	*Three cases of scarlet fever reported.*
23 Dec:	*Only 15 children came to school owing to the snow.*

1939

9 Jan:	*School reopened after Christmas holidays. There were present: B. Bale, F. Stark, P. Crane, B. Stark, C. Jewell, G. Smith, E. Greed, B. Baker, J. Duddridge, F. Crane, A. Stark, J. Reed, J. Coles, F. Smith, E. Smith, J. Bellamy, M. Gibbons, E. Jewell, M. Woodman, J. Touchin, P. Bailey, S. Stevens, J. Leaworthy, H. Reed, D. Smith, A. Duddridge, D. Coles, A. Taylor, B. Leaworthy – 29 in senior and junior classes. David Smith, N. Woodman, R. Colman, R. Payne, T. Stark, A. Smith, R. Scott, E. Watts, B. Touchin, P. Stevens – 10 in infant room.*
25–26 Jan:	*School closed owing to snow.*
5 May:	*School time-table altered to meet trains on account of bus strike.*
3 Sept:	*War declared.*
25 Sept:	*There are 74 children on registers – 47 village children and 27 evacuees.*
2 Oct:	*Mr A.J. Mason began work in this school to assist with the evacuation children.*

1940

19 Jan:	*School closed on account of snow.*
19 June:	*Twenty-three evacuee children were allocated to the village. Combe Cottage has been taken for an annexe.*
3 Sept:	*School reopened after summer holidays. Miss Rowe, LCC teacher, joined the staff.*
26 Nov:	*There are 101 children in the school – 47 Crowcombe children and 54 evacuees.*
20 Dec:	*The Women's Institute gave a party to the Crowcombe and evacuated children up to the age of 14 years – the total number was 169.*

1941

9 June:	*Dairy class: Miss Lewis had a class of 12 children – six boys and six girls.*
20 June:	*School closed from today until 30 June for postponed Whitsuntide holidays in order that children may help with the hay harvest.*
7 July:	*Sports meeting in Crowcombe Recreation Ground organised by the Forces billeted in the village.*
3 Oct:	*School closed for potato lifting holiday.*

1942

23 March:	*School closed owing to cold – no coke available.*

1943

24 Feb:	*Death of the Revd Prebendary H. Christian Young, Rector and chairman of the school managers.*
28 June:	*Children in the charge of one teacher visited whortleberry hills and picked 42lbs for jam.*
29 June:	*Jam-making – the senior girls made 84lbs of jam using 49lbs of fruit and 49lbs of sugar.*
29 Nov:	*School meals began from Wiveliscombe centre.*
25 Dec:	*Evacuees entertained by USA troops for Christmas dinner at the camp at Crowcombe Heathfield.*

1944

6 June:	*D-Day – Allied invasion of Nazi-occupied Europe at Normandy beaches.*
13 July:	*Whortleberry picking for jam.*
14 July:	*Jam-making in school.*
20 July:	*Picking whortleberries for sale to pay for jam sugar.*
21 Sept:	*Picked blackberries near Recreation Ground.*
22 Sept:	*Cookery girls made blackberry and apple jam.*
9 Oct:	*Four school overalls delivered to Mrs Smith and Mrs Tuckfield (two each) for serving of school meals.*

1945

2 March:	*London examinations: Doris Cunningham senr, I. Horton, Keith Baker, Leonard Grainger and Eileen Skipp.*

CROWCOMBE

Crowcombe schoolchildren with their Nativity model, 1968. Left to right: Christopher Brewer, Ruth Chidgey, Adrian Salt, Peter Chidley, Ian Fisher.

Children engrossed in a game of Scrabble at Crowcombe CE VA First School, 1969. Left to right: Robert England, Simon Fisher, Ian Fisher, John Dyer.

Concert group at Crowcombe CE VA First School, 1969. Left to right: Rachael Gill, Coralie Brewer, Kathryn Chilcott, Louisa West, Susan Gill.

Pupils enjoying a lesson at Crowcombe CE VA First School, 1970. Left to right: Philip Norman, Storm Brewer, John Dyer, Kathryn Chilcott, Jacinth Mackie.

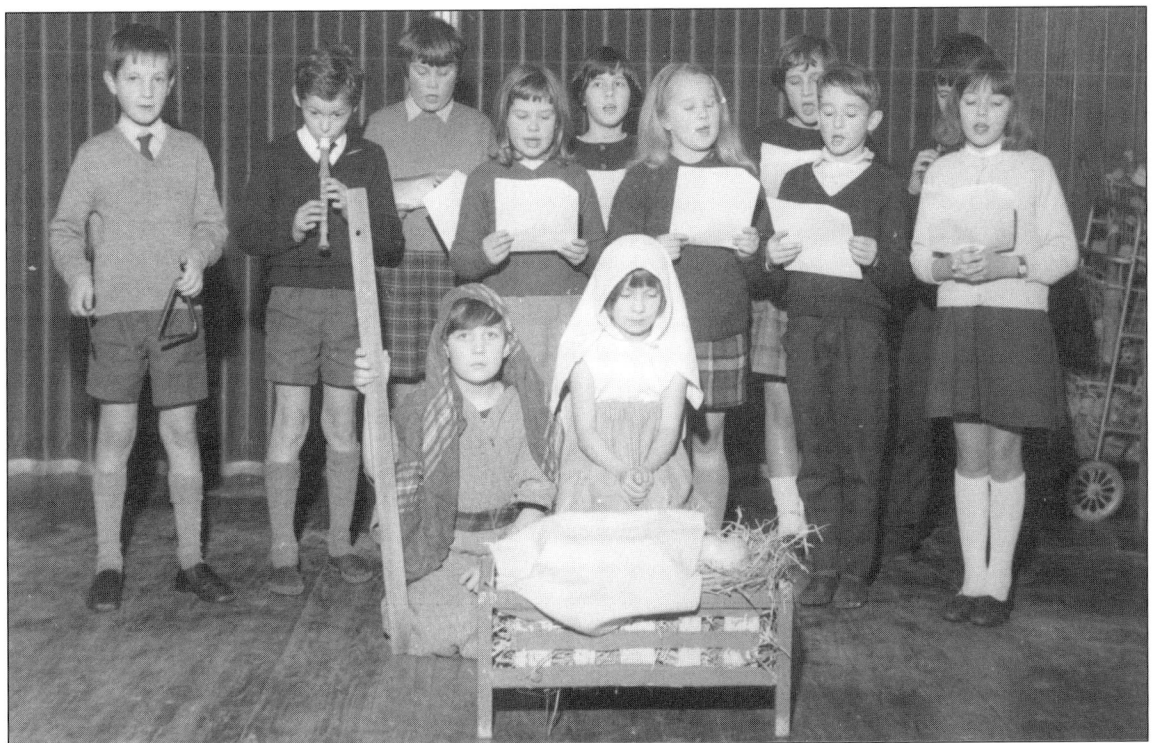

Crowcombe CE School, c.1968. Left to right, back row: Stephen Barnes, Ashley Baker, Susan Herniman, Jacinth Mackie, Diane Jenkins, Kathryn Chilcott, Susan Jenkins, Leslie Holman, ?, Valerie Kingston; front: Philip Norman, Ruth Chidgey.

10/11 May:	VE Days holiday.
5 Sept:	School reopened after summer holidays, including two VJ Days holiday.

1946
21 Jan:	School closed for five days owing to cold and influenza.
17 May:	Scholarship examination – Jean Needham and Edmund Venner sitting.

1947
29 Jan–7 Feb:	School closed on account of severe weather.
5–7 March:	School closed owing to return of blizzard conditions – no buses running through village.

1948
26 April:	Half-day's holiday for silver wedding of King George VI and Queen Elizabeth.
6 Sept:	Senior children transferred to Williton School.
31 Dec:	Headmistress resigned.

1949
6 Jan:	Mrs Reynish begins duties as headmistress.
11 Feb:	Scholarship examination, four children present – Brian Lewis absent through illness.
22 Feb:	New Wiveliscombe kitchen supervisor called, had dinner with staff and children, admitted that plate rack was useless for warming plates – dinner very cold, as always – promised to speak to organiser. Valerie Ash had nasty cut near right eye; she was swinging on desk.
3 March:	Very good dinner today, cheese and raw salad. Children thought cabbage was lettuce!
18 March:	Brian Lewis sat the scholarship examination. Great excitement – PT shoes arrived!
7 April:	R. very rude to Mrs Hunt.
18 May:	Mr Brewer complained about children in car – two girls exceedingly rude to him.
23 May:	One new child – Peter Thorne.
22 June:	Brian Lewis and Ruth Jarrett were successful in obtaining scholarships into a grammar school.

1950
5 Jan:	School reopened – one new child admitted, Ivor Berryman.
1 Feb:	I had to punish R.R. for being impertinent to Miss Bray.
8 March:	Pat Moxman fell in playground, cut hand and knee.
24 April:	Number on books 51.
26 April:	Admitted Mary Routley.
23 June:	Julia Payne and Gweneth Owen have free places in grammar school.
27 July:	Boys dug potatoes, scraped them and we cooked them for dinner.
28 July:	Rector called to wish children who were leaving goodbye – Janet Scott, Gweneth Owen, Julia Payne, Desmond Venner.

1951
7 March:	I punished D.B. for chewing gum in school after repeated warnings.
1 May:	Mrs Trollope-Bellew invited the school to a picnic tea and games at the Court.
22 June:	James Bull and Lewis Cavill have free places to grammar school.
17 July:	I took children to the Recreation Ground for sports and games – Hazel Labbe fell and hurt her back.
9 Sept:	Revd Peter Birkett called and spoke to the children.
13 Sept:	Electricians fixed line to school.
10 Dec:	Staff had no dinner – not enough meat for children.

1952
20 May:	A girl very rude to Mrs Tuckfield – I caned her.
27 June:	Sonia Webber given a free place to grammar school.

1953
17 March:	Major and Mrs Trollope-Bellew distributed the Carew Charity, £12.17s.6d. Four children made full attendance for 1952. Mrs Trollope-Bellew brought baby Anthony in.
27 April:	Admitted Bridget Webber.
22 May:	School closed until 4 June for Whitsuntide and Coronation.
16 June:	Colin Norman had a nasty cut over right eye – after bathing, I took him to Dr Meyers.

1954
4 Jan:	School reopened – 61 children on books.
1 Feb:	No water in school – water supplied by Mrs Bale. The coke sent useless for the stoves – room very cold.
8 Feb:	No water, lavatories still frozen up. Water carried in by staff and older boys from neighbours.
19 Oct:	I had to punish R.L. and M.W. for rudeness at the dining table.

1955
14 Jan:	Nineteen children in school owing to deep snow – closed mid-day.
27 Jan:	Josie Owen fell in playground, hurt her wrist.
4 March:	Mr Duddridge attended to burst pipes and lavatories' tanks. Lavatories flushed for first time since 22 February. No meat or pudding for teaching and canteen staff.
13 May:	Josie Owen called for interview re free place in grammar school.
7 June:	R.L., F.D. and M.G. very rude in the dining room – Miss Bray very upset.
9 June:	I was asked by the police inspector to go to Mrs Tuckfield, the school cleaner, to break the news of her husband's death by accident at the quarry.

CROWCOMBE

Crowcombe CE VA First School in the 1980s. Left to right, back row: Miss Laird, Mr Hallmark (head teacher), Helen Chidley, Laurence Strong, Tessa Lamacraft, Joanne Packer, Piers Montaque, Christopher Hayes, Graham Gibbs, Christopher Lewis, Mrs Bindon, Mrs Betts; middle: Sally Ward, Ian Saunders, Kate Little, Joanne Osborne, Tracey Chiplin, Stuart Bailey, ? Cavill, Natalie Knell, David Harbour, Paula Chidley, Reuben Goodwell, Mark Duddridge; front: Sally Richmond, Hanna Lamacraft, Nathaniel Hawthorne, Bernard Knell, Sandra Parsons, Katie Ward, Rebecca Swain, Penny Gibbs, James Strong.

Crowcombe schoolchildren take a peep into the past in a joint venture with other local first schools in 'Operation Backalong', c.1985. Left to right: Richard Strong, Rebecca Holmes, Jack Lamacraft, Charlotte Merriman, Mark Cartwright, Natalie Swannack, Emma Saunders, Ben Woollard.

Crowcombe CE VA First School Nativity, 1986.

Crowcombe School music group, c.1993. Left to right, back row: Laura Webber, Nicola Penn, Mr David Ellery, Amy Lewis, Tessa Appleby; front: Chloe Reed, James Greswell, Jennifer Sully.

Crowcombe CE VA First School catchball team, 1994. Left to right, back row: Katy Gover, Dee Rickward, Helen Druitt, Laura Webber; front: Beth Pascall, Tessa Rosling, Amy Lewis.

Crowcombe CE VA First School four-a-side indoor football team, 1994. Left to right: Thomas Knell, Brendan Ahern, Paul Marks, William Tempest.

Reception age group at Crowcombe CE VA First School, 1995–96. Left to right: William Staniland, Andrew Miles, Matthew Hatfield, Stephen Weston, Sarah Ash, Rebecca Chidley, Katy Burnell.

The 125th anniversary of Crowcombe CE VA First School, 1997. The children and staff were all attired in Victorian dress. The head, Mrs Barbara Beer, is seated in the centre.

Visit of Bishop Jim to bless a new classroom at Crowcombe CE VA First School, 1999. Left to right, back row: Ben Rutt, Ben Druitt, Iona Tilly, Kristie Cockayne, Luke Trimmings, Allen Ross, Eleanor Morley, Heidi Burnell; middle: Clemmie Tilly, Sophie Townsend, Rebecca Trimmings, Bishop Jim Thompson, Issie Hatfield, Theo Tennant; front: James Bebb, David Burden, ?, Edward Hatfield, Jonathan Morley.

Crowcombe CE VA First School, at the time of the new millennium. Left to right, back row: Mrs Hellier, Rebecca Trimmings, Heidi Burnell, Andrew Ross, Eleanor Morley, Mark Trimmings, Thomas Pumphrey, Katy Burnell, Matthew Hatfield, ?, Andrew Miles, Mrs Ashwell; third row: David Burden, Harry Hudson, Theo Tennant, Clemmie Tilley, Sarah Ash, ? Druitt, Iona Tilley, Natasha Mowatt; second row: Ben Rutt, Sophie Townsend, Edward Hatfield, Luke Moffatt, Mrs B.A. Beer (head), Miss Bond, Jonathan Morley, James Bebb, Michael ?, Edward Morris; front: Jonathan Bebb, Michaela Hudson, Isabel Hatfield, Noah Tilley.

CROWCOMBE

Class Two of Crowcombe CE VA First School celebrate the school's full- and part-time staff achieving the coveted Investor in People Award, held by head teacher Anthea Deane, 2004. The national award requires organisations to demonstrate their ability to maximise staff potential and recognise their contribution towards continued success. Clockwise from bottom left: William Chester, Jamie Hole, Hannah Foy, Sophie Gregson-Brown, Alistair Weldon, Luke Mowat, Ryan Bailey-Vaughan, Gemma Webber, Ashley Barons, Jordan Langley, Lucy Rutt, Fergus Napper.

Left: *Crowcombe CE VA First School Nativity play, 2000. Amongst those pictured are: Lily Russell, Emily Webber, Harry Hudson, Eleanor Morley, Issie, Edward and Matthew Hatfield, David Burden, Jonathan Morley, Jonathan Bebb, Edward Morris, James Bebb, Sophie Townsend, Theo Tennant, Luke Trimmings, Madeline Hudson, Lucy Rutt, Thomas Morris, Sophie Gregson-Brown, Luke Mowat, Fergus Napier, Clemmie Tilly.*

Left: *Mrs Beer's retirement as head of Crowcombe CE VA First School, July 2000. Left to right: Hannah Brooks (past pupil), James Bebb (youngest pupil), Mrs Beer, Katy Burnell (oldest pupil).*

Right: *Celebrating the Golden Jubilee of Queen Elizabeth II at Crowcombe CE VA First School in 2002. Left to right, back row: Celia Bebb, Helen Hatfield, ?, Rosie MacDonald, Lucy Rutt, Henry MacDonald, Michaela Hudson, Richard Morris; standing in front: Jamie Hole, Thomas Morris.*

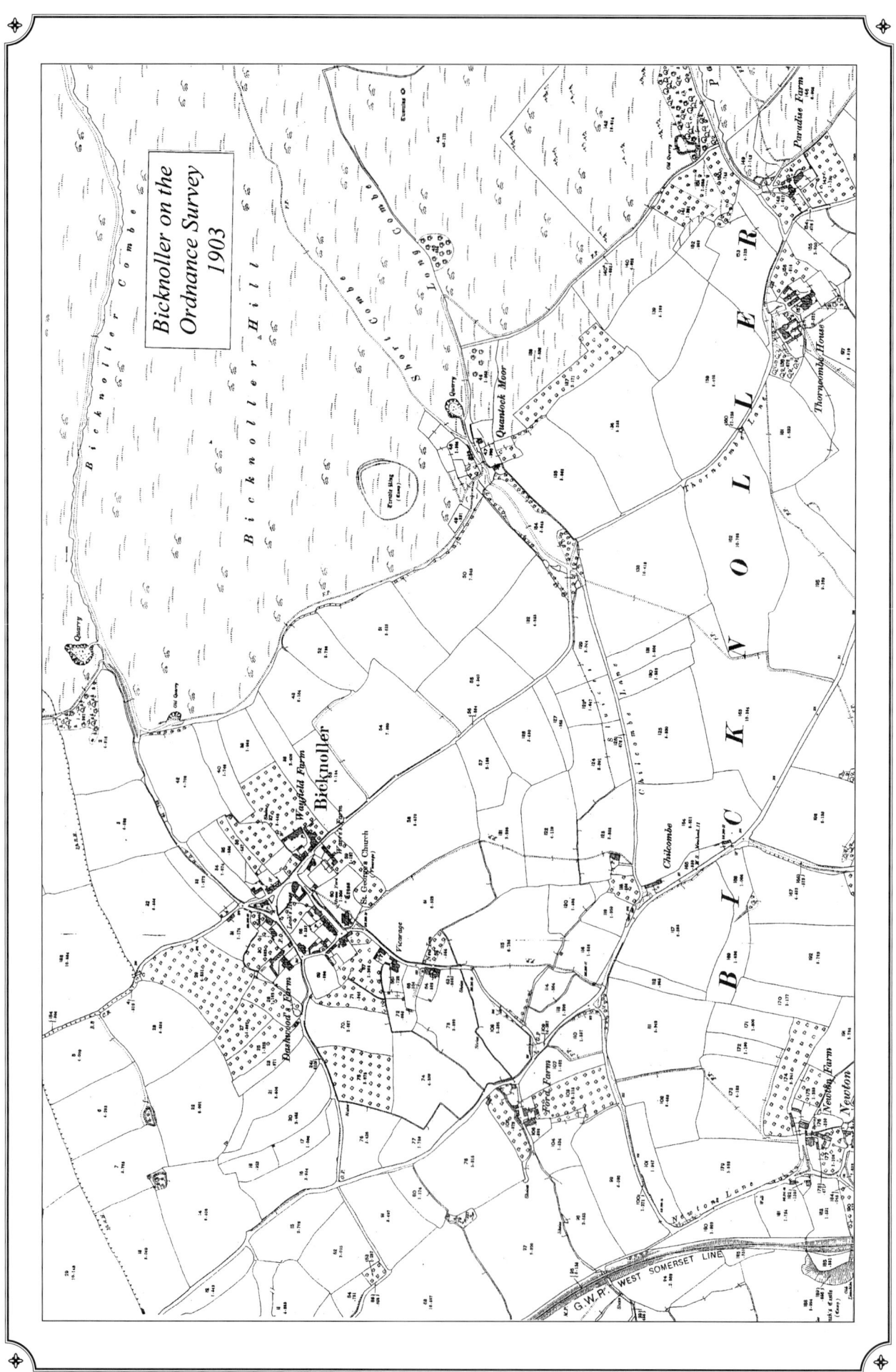

Chapter 2

Bicknoller

Without doubt Bicknoller is one of the Quantock's prettiest villages, where old thatched cottages, dating mainly from the sixteenth to eighteenth centuries, mingle with modern houses and bungalows. Tiny streams, half hidden by wild flowers, ferns and grasses, run down from the hills alongside the narrow roads. Lying on the south-western slopes of the Quantocks, the parish is three miles south-east of Williton, with the Doniford stream forming the boundary with Sampford Brett and Stogumber. Halsway was added from Stogumber in 1883 to form the civil parish of Bicknoller, which in 2002 had a population peak of 390. The village, off from the main A358 road, is a tranquil place today, but was much noisier 100 years ago when a big stone quarry was working on its outskirts. Stone was quarried at Woolston and Newton by the mid-fifteenth century, and Woolston quarry, with a limekiln, was still open in 1904.

A permanent prehistoric settlement may be represented by Trendle Ring on the slope of Bicknoller Hill. It is thought that the name 'Trendle' is of Anglo-Saxon origin meaning circle. About a mile lower down is another earthwork, of which very few traces remain, called Turk's Castle. There were recorded settlements at Newton and Woolston in the eleventh century, and Bicknoller is first mentioned by name in 1243. The name Bicknoller has two possible derivations – one is Bica's Alder (Bica is a Saxon name) and the other is from the ancient British words Bychan (small) and Alwar (treasury), Roman coins having been found in these parts. The present hamlet of Newton may derive its name from the presence there of a Domesday mill. Established settlements by the early-fourteenth century were Yard, Chapmanscombe, Chilcombe, Upcott, Thorncombe, Cottiford, Ford and Culverhayes. Two parallel routes between the Quantock scarp and the Doniford stream seem to have been the road pattern, with lanes from Bicknoller village to the outlying hamlets. The lower road became the main route between Taunton and Minehead and was turnpiked in 1807. In 1862 the West Somerset Railway was opened and its route was cut through the parish, involving road alterations and new buildings at Woolston and Yard, but no station stop.

Bicknoller is not mentioned in the Domesday Book, but the parish consisted of two estates in 1066 –

Church Lane, Bicknoller, c.1905.

Trendle Ring.

Woolston held by Britmar and Newton held by Alviet. Both were held by William de Mohun by 1086 and until 1620 or later continued to be held of the honour of Dunster. Agnes, William's great-granddaughter and wife of William de Windsor, inherited the estates. After her husband's death, Agnes divided the estates, giving half to Godehuda, wife of Nicholas Rolland. After Nicholas's death, Godehuda brought her land to her second husband, Richard de Wayville, who was holding an estate in 1243 described as half the manor of Bicknoller. The other half of the manor was probably retained by Agnes until her death, upon which in the late-thirteenth century there was much litigation involving her descendants. Godehuda's sons by her two marriages, William Rolland and Henry de Wayville, and the Windsor family were the main claimants. Disputes continued until 1291 when the Wayvilles were awarded half the manor, and in 1303 the property was shared between Richard de Windsor and James de Wayville. Land was given for three masses a year for Henry de Wayvile and his family during Edward I's reign. The Wayvilles or Wayviles were a Norman family who appeared at Bicknoller at the beginning of the thirteenth century. The name was spelt in many different ways before the introduction of printing when the name settled down to Wavell. Lord Wavell, of Second World War fame, was a member of this family.

Richard de Windsor granted his half manor to Robert de Cormailles in 1327, and Robert's brother Roger gave it to the Chapter of Wells in 1330. The Wayvilles continued to hold the other half of the manor until Richard Wayville of Rodmell (Sussex), who died in 1417, left his estate to be sold. It was obtained by the executors of Nicholas Bubwith (d.1424), Bishop of Bath and Wells, and it was acquired by the Wells Chapter in 1430 until 1857 when they were succeeded by the Ecclesiastical (later Church) Commissioners. Called Wayfield, the manor-house was let from 1622 or possibly earlier, and was occupied by successive manor bailiffs, including the Bickhams, from the seventeenth until the late-nineteenth century.

The manor-house was built by James de Wayville in 1286 as a single-storey longhouse with a central walk-through chimney, the owner's family living on

Mr Charles Herbert Greswell, who bought Manor Farm (now known as Wayvile House) in 1898.

one side of the chimney and the serfs on the other. A second storey was built in the sixteenth century, and at the turn of the twentieth century the roof was raised a further two feet and an elegant staircase and windows added to the rear of the property. In 1898 Mr Charles Herbert Greswell bought it from the Church Commissioners, and members of the Greswell family still reside there. It is now known as Wayvile House. The Church Commissioners were still lords of the manor of Bicknoller until 1954 when they sold their rights to Williton RDC.

Agnes de Windsor granted in fee in 1221 to Richard de Wechesford and his wife Maud an estate formerly belonging to Richard of Thorncombe. This probably formed part of the lands Agnes gave to her daughter Godehuda, for in 1227 she and her husband Richard de Wayville held 1.5 virgate in Thorncombe. In

Manor Farm (now known as Wayvile), Bicknoller, c.1895.

Aerial view of Thorncombe House and surrounds.

1281–82 Simon Brett was lord of Thorncombe and by 1356 the Brett family had a substantial holding at Thorncombe. In the following century the manor comprised lands and tenements in Bicknoller, Stogumber and Crowcombe, the estate continuing in the hands of the Brett family throughout the fifteenth and sixteenth centuries. In 1609, Alexander Brett, then living in Lincolnshire, sold the manor to John Sweeting. The Sweeting family already held considerable estates in Bicknoller, but their principal residence had been at Sampford Brett. John Sweeting moved to Thorncombe, where his descendants lived for over 150 years. It would appear that the family were clothiers who, having invested in land at Bicknoller, Sampford Brett, Torweston and Stogumber, were able to rise to the ranks of the gentry. Joseph Sweeting III died without issue in 1772 and was the last Sweeting to live at Thorncombe, the estate being sold and subsequently divided. Thorncombe House was owned by the Norris family for most of the nineteenth century, and in more recent years by the late Mr Arthur Capewell, QC, and presently by Mr Julian Luttrell. A house at Thorncombe was mentioned in 1334 when an oratory was licensed to John Brett for a year. Thorncombe House was built in 1744, the five-bay front being rebuilt in the nineteenth century and additions made to the south and rear later in the century.

Many of Bicknoller's old houses are still called by the names of the families who originally lived in them – Dashwoods, Gatchells, Blakes, Locks, Ford, Jenkyns and Saffins. One of the village's most famous sons was Roger Mander, master of Balliol College, Oxford, in 1687. Another name associated with Bicknoller is artist John William North, ARA, RWS (1842–1924). He was a landscape painter in watercolour and occasionally oil. London born, North lived in Somerset from 1868, at first with Fred Walker at Halsway Manor and from this stage on his landscapes are almost invariably taken from the Quantock Hills and neighbouring countryside. Cardinal Beaufort was also associated with Halsway, where he had a hunting lodge.

Bicknoller's beautiful little Parish Church of St George is built of local red sandstone with Ham stone dressings. It possibly originates from the thirteenth century, but there were many additions, including the tower, in the fifteenth century. Originally a chapel of Stogumber, from 1368 or earlier the chaplain or curate was appointed and paid by the vicar of that parish. A unique feature of the chancel is the original medieval stone altar, which was rediscovered undamaged. Mr E.A. Greswell, one of the churchwardens, happened to strike it with his scythe while cutting long grass in the churchyard. It was restored in the 1950s. Other striking features of the church are the fan-vaulted screen and carved bench-ends, some being very fine specimens of early-Tudor type. In 1930 some important discoveries were made at the church during architectural restoration when four ancient windows were uncovered after being blocked up in the walls for 100 years or more. One was at the east end, one at the west end and two in the chancel. Five new bench-ends were placed at the front of the north aisle in 1932. Another notable feature of the church is its range of stained-glass windows. The window at the west end of the nave

Dashwoods, Bicknoller.

Clarence House, Bicknoller.

St George's Church, Bicknoller.

Left: *A 1932 bench-end with a fine representation of Bicknoller Church, showing the little yew tree growing on the church tower.*

Right: *A relatively modern bench-end portraying the village stocks under the yew tree in Bicknoller churchyard and a stag and fox at the bottom.*

The interior of Bicknoller Parish Church before the installation of electricity.

The organ in its new position in Bicknoller Parish Church, 2005.

BICKNOLLER

The village stocks sheltering under an ancient yew tree in Bicknoller churchyard. The stocks were given new wood early in the twentieth century, but the iron frame is original.

Snow scene at Bicknoller churchyard showing the headstones of members of the Bickham family.

was replaced in 1952 by a new one in memory of Mr H.B. Mayor; an interesting feature of this window is a tiny portrait of Mr Mayor's little dog. The tower contains five bells, one of them pre-Reformation (1420–60). Still standing in the churchyard is the fourteenth-century churchyard cross, though the original cross portion at the top of the shaft was replaced in about 1920. At the top of the churchyard is the village pound, where straying animals were shut in until claimed by their owners. Behind the church is a row of seven headstones in memory of the Bickham family, who resided at Wayvile and kept greyhounds, inviting unlimited numbers of guests to organised coursing, preceded by enormous champagne breakfasts. There are three old yew trees near the church, one of which shelters the village stocks.

Morning and afternoon services were attended by 72 and 145 people respectively in 1851. Daily services and weekly celebrations were held at Bicknoller and weekly services at Woolston from 1867–69. From 1869–77 it was found that the Woolston services were better attended than those of the Parish Church. There was a Church House at Bicknoller, but by 1580 it had been acquired by the parish as a poorhouse. There was a small curate's cottage in 1815 and a wing was added in 1868 to the two-storeyed thatched building which stood in the village street south-west of the church. After a fire in 1883 the wing alone survived; a new house was built and continued as the Vicarage until 1956 when it was sold. In 1962 a house was built in Trendle Lane to replace it. Dr Temple, a former Archbishop of

Members of the Bickham family, along with their retainers and pets, c.1885.

The fireplace at the New Inn (now the Bicknoller Inn), c.1930s.

Canterbury, regularly took his holidays in the area and worshipped at Bicknoller during 1933–44. The living is now part of the Quantock Towers Benefice.

In 1669 Nonconformists were meeting at several houses in the parish, and in 1734 the newly-erected house of William Cornish was licensed as a Presbyterian meeting-house. Wesleyan Methodists decided to introduce preaching into Bicknoller in 1834, but the scheme was abandoned in the following year. The Wesleyans held an afternoon meeting at Cottiford in 1894 and at Woolston between 1895–97. The Salvation Army held meetings in Bicknoller and Woolston in 1883.

An infant school was started at Bicknoller in 1828, followed by a day school in 1832, and by 1835 they taught the combined total of 32 children. There was a Sunday school held in the church in 1846–47 attended by 42 children. In 1855 the Vestry rejected the vicar's motion to start a school for the 'labouring classes', the educational wants of the parish then being said to be deplorable. However, in 1863 the Wells Chapter gave a site for a school. By 1881 there were 106 pupils enrolled, but by 1893 there were only 35 children on the books. The average attendance had fallen to 14 in 1905, and the school was closed in December 1911. The building was later used as a Post Office, and for community activities until 1954, when a Village Hall was built on adjacent land left by Henry Bickersteth Mayor for that purpose and also for a playing-field. The old school is now a private residence.

There were two licensed victuallers in 1736, and the Bicknoller Inn (formerly the New Inn) is mentioned in 1841, but could be of earlier origin. It appears to have had a somewhat chequered career, as in earlier times it was a general shop and Post Office as well as an inn. At the time of Queen Victoria's Golden Jubilee in 1887 there was a Tudor fireplace in the inn, which points to the possibility of the inn itself being of Tudor origin. Attached to the fireplace were a large baking oven and an enormous cupboard, large enough to conceal three men. The purpose of this cupboard was to smoke and dry bacon. In 1890 the fireplace was built in and a modern kitchen range substituted. During renovations in 1933 the Tudor fireplace was again brought to light, and the old oven and bacon cupboard were intact and unharmed. In 1900 the coach-house attached to the inn was demolished. This was hundreds of years old and showed every indication of having been the original inn.

Bicknoller Inn, 2004.

The almhouses, Woolston, c.1920.

As well as the inn there was a Post Office which was under the supervision of the Jennings family for many years and later a Post Office was run by Mrs Spark in the old school. There was also a little shop in the village under the proprietorship of Mrs Lewis which sold groceries and newspapers.

Agriculture was the main economic stability of the parish, and from the seventeenth century to the mid-nineteenth there was a balance between arable and pasture farming. Giles Sweeting, of Wayfield, who died in 1692, had a malt-house, salting house, milkhouse, horses, 12 cattle, 232 sheep, 12 pigs, ricks of wheat, barley, oats, hay and peas, and an assortment of implements. The total value of the inventory of his goods was £317. The main crops in 1883 were wheat, beans, barley, oats and turnips.

Common land played a significant part in the farming of the parish, and in 1838 there were 340 acres of common land at Woolston Moor, Bicknoller Hill and Quantock Moor, the last settled by squatters. From the early-seventeenth century weavers, serge weavers, dyers and clothiers occur in the parish. There was a mill on the Newton estate in 1086, and there were also later mills at Chapmanscombe, Thorncombe and Cottiford. From the mid-nineteenth century there were clothing clubs, and a lending library in 1877. Tennis, fives and bowls were played in the sixteenth and seventeenth centuries, and wassailing on Old Twelfth Night continued at least until 1870.

Queen Victoria's Jubilees were celebrated by feasting and jollification, with triumphal arches decorating the village on both occasions. Part of the celebrations of the Golden Jubilee was a decorated farm wagon drawn by a team of 10 shire horses. Each horse came from the different farms of the parish and was led by its carter. At the Diamond Jubilee in 1897 the inhabitants partook in relays of a wonderful repast set out in the beautifully decorated tithe barn at Dashwoods, which is a house of early-seventeenth-century origin. The Dashwood family (after whom the house was named – the previous house name, if any, is unknown) came from Vellow Wood Farm in the early-eighteenth century.

The Bartholomew Thomas almshouses at Woolston were founded under a bequest by Lucy Thomas, who died in 1902. She gave £3,000 for four almshouses for poor Protestants of 55 or over of good character who were unable to work. The almshouses were completed in 1905 by J. Chibbett & Sons of Williton, six old cottages being demolished on the site to make way for them. In 1987 the almshouses were renovated by their charitable trust under the chairmanship of Mrs Elizabeth Darke.

The parish became part of the Williton Poor Law Union in 1836, and remained in the Williton Rural District until inclusion in the West Somerset District in 1974; it has a Parish Council. The village, which has grown much since the Second World War, now has the benefit of a community shop and Post Office, and much use is made of the fine Village Hall for social and formal occasions. Bicknoller is justly proud of its prestigious annual Flower Show, which has been described as the 'little Chelsea' of West Somerset.

Opening of new village Post Office and shop

John Lees (chairman of the Parish Council) cutting the ribbon to officially open the new Post Office and shop at Bicknoller in April 1995. The former Post Office had closed four years previously and before its renovation the new premises, sited near the Village Hall, had been a dilapidated old barn. The project was financed by interest-free loans and donations from villagers and a grant from the Rural Development Commission. The internal fitting-out was completed mainly by volunteer helpers and many of the fittings were donated. It is managed, as a community amenity, by a non-profit-making friendly society, supported by 130 shareholders from the village. All the staff in both the shop and Post Office sections are unpaid volunteers and maintain it as a thriving concern. Left to right: John Barraclough, John Multon, Elma Trickett, Michael Sutton, Rita Seamons, John Lees, Tom King (then the local MP), Liz Antliff-Clark, Bill Pumphrey. In 2005 an anniversary party was held to celebrate 10 years' successful trading by the Post Office and shop.

Gathering of villagers and guests to celebrate the opening of the new Bicknoller Post Office and shop, 1995. Left to right, back row: Jeanne Barraclough, Percy Maine, Anna Ninnes (holding Rick), Jean Wigley, Gill Goodland, Tom King MP, Paula Ninnes; sitting: Mary Maine, ?, Doris Gay, Valerie Broomfield.

The dilapidated barn before its renovation into the new Post Office and shop at Bicknoller.

Norah Linck giving the vote of thanks at the opening of Bicknoller Post Office and shop, 1995.

Bill Pumphrey and Mary Rudram busy in Bicknoller's Post Office and shop.

Women's Institute

Bicknoller Women's Institute, 1946. Bicknoller Women's Institute was founded in 1946, its first president being Mrs Marion Thomas. There were 72 founder members, amongst whom were Joyce Barber, Olive Davis, Gertrude Jennings and Mary Maine. Membership reached its peak in 1948 when it stood at 85, and over its first 50 years there were 16 presidents, 19 secretaries and 12 treasurers, the longest-serving president being Mrs Marion Baxter (13 years). Unfortunately at the time of writing the local WI is disbanded, but it is to be hoped that it will be restarted in the future.

Celebrating the 50th anniversary of Bicknoller Women's Institute, March 1996. Left to right, back row: B. Williams, Rose Fish, Jeanette Bole, Sheila Clifton, Maggie Pumphrey, Betty Limmington, Gladys Fillary, Eve Griffin, Babs Billington, Mary Rudram; third row: Jeanne Kendall, Leslie Wood, Doris Gay, Valerie Broomfield, Ann Sutton, Rita Seamons, Jean Thompson; second row: Elma Trickett, Del Snell, Mary Stockham, Louise Jeffreys, Brenda Newton, Molly Farmer, Margaret Tizzard; front: Eileen Toal, Joyce Barber, Mary Maine, Norah Linck, Queenie Payne.

Members of Bicknoller Women's Institute celebrating their first 50 years in 1996. Left to right, standing: Norah Linck, ?, Margaret Pritchard, ?, Dorothy Wilson, Elma Trickett, Mary Maine, Molly Farmer, Joyce Barber, Eileen Toal, Olive Davis, Brenda Newton; front, sitting: ?, Louise Jeffreys.

Bicknoller WI and friends support the British Olympic Appeal, 1984. Left to right: B. Newton, J. Thompson, D. Snell, E. Grainger, K. Marriott, A. Marriott.

Bicknoller Women's Institute, 2000. Left to right, back row: B. Willcock, M. Rudram, M. de Sausmarez, G. Fillary, C. Hall, C. Darke, L. Wood, C. Clifton, D. Gay, E. Griffin, P. Chandler, R. Fish, R. Seamons; front: N. Linck, A. Williams, B. Billington, J. Thompson, E. Toal, J. Towler, A. Raisey, M. Tizzard, M. Maine, M. Stockham, L. Jeffreys.

Bicknoller Flower Show

An early Bicknoller Flower Show, c.1959.

George and Hetty Touchin and Queenie Payne admiring exhibits at a 1960s Bicknoller Flower Show.

Exhibits at Bicknoller Flower Show, 1963.

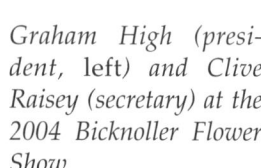

Graham High (president, left) and Clive Raisey (secretary) at the 2004 Bicknoller Flower Show.

Tina Pendray (chairman) among the blooms at the 2004 Bicknoller Flower Show.

Admirers at the 2004 Bicknoller Flower Show.

BICKNOLLER

Parish and People

Aerial photograph of Bicknoller, c.1970.

Halsway Manor, c.1910. It dates from before 1066 and was rebuilt in the 1400s with further redevelopment in the late 1800s. It is now owned by the Halsway Manor Society and is home to Britain's only permanent residential folk-music centre.

The late Mr E.J. Mardon, BA, LLB, formerly of Halsway Manor. He was a barrister-at-law of the Inner Temple and had a distinguished 25-year career in the Indian Civil Service.

The late Betty Mardon, formerly of Halsway Manor, who joined the Red Cross in 1936 and obtained her first nursing certificate that year. It was the beginning of a life in the Red Cross that was largely dedicated to the service of others, both at home and abroad. Although her first love was West Somerset, Betty was well travelled and always made a point of contacting the local Red Cross wherever she happened to be, whether in Africa, Canada, the USA, or European countries. A special favourite was the Red Cross Children's Centre at Dagoretti in Kenya. In between her travels Betty was an indefatigable worker in her community for the Red Cross – a fact reflected in her rise from an ordinary member to fully qualified Voluntary Aid Detachment (VAD) instructor, West Somerset Divisional secretary, Commandant Stogumber Centre and West Divisional president in 1950. In 1955 she moved up to Somerset County branch and the position of deputy branch president, and finally in 1974 she was made honorary vice-president of the county branch. Along the way Betty collected innumerable certificates, long service badges, a branch commendation and a certificate of honour and life membership.

Queenie Payne (left) and Betty Mardon in the 1980s.

Local detachment of the Red Cross who won the Maud Mardon Cup in 1954. Left to right, back row: Mrs Hume, Miss Mullins, Mrs Horsey, Miss Jones; sitting: Miss Pearce, Miss Betty Mardon (divisional president and commandant Somerset/60), Mrs Q. Payne.

Queenie Payne sitting pretty on a scooter at Halsway Manor in the 1950s.

Meet of the Quantock Staghounds at Halsway Manor in the late 1940s.

A ladies' gathering at Halsway Manor, in the 1930s. Among those pictured are: Mrs Mardon, Mrs Hettie Touchin, Mrs Queenie Payne, Mrs Jewell, Miss Hilda Chidley.

Children evacuated from Bristol to Halsway Manor in 1940. Mr Mardon and Betty are at the back and Mrs Mardon is sitting in the front nursing a toddler.

Village group at Bicknoller to celebrate the millennium.

BICKNOLLER

The Rutt family and helpers relaxing at The Paddocks, Bicknoller, after a hard day's harvesting, 1936.

Ann, Robin and Michael Rutt with relatives at Bicknoller during harvest time, 1943.

Harvesting at Bicknoller, c.1960. Left to right: Spencer Lyddon, Gary Bowerman, Mr Criddle.

Leonard and Frances Rutt of Bicknoller with daughter Ann and twins Michael (left) and Robin, 1938.

Mrs Frances Rutt with daughter Ann at a baby competition, 1934.

Frances Davis (later Mrs Rutt of Bicknoller) in Girl Guide uniform astride a cow, c.1920s.

Ann Rutt, of Bicknoller, with a Guernsey calf, c.1940.

Olive Mabel Davis, who resided at Bicknoller for many years, in her Easter bonnet.

Special Constable Michael Rutt, c.1970s.

Robin Rutt in his uniform as cruise purser. Twin son of the late Mr and Mrs L.A. Rutt, of Bicknoller, Robin was appointed cruise director of the Union Castle Line's ss Reina del Mar *in 1966, when he had the job of keeping some 1,000 passengers entertained on the 21,000-ton liner. Robin and his twin brother Michael are old boys of Huish's Grammar School (now Richard Huish College), in Taunton. Their grandfather was the late Mr H.E. Davis, formerly of Monksilver.*

Joe and Bessie Sully, of Woolston, at the time of their golden wedding in the 1960s. They resided at Railway Cottage, Joe being a ganger on the railway for many years. He was also a keen marksman, shooting for Bicknoller British Legion Rifle Club.

Members of Bicknoller British Legion Rifle Club in the 1950s. Left to right: Walter Welsher, ?, Albert Berry, Lewis Gimblett, Wilfred Milton, Joe Sully.

Four of the Bicknoller British Legion Rifle team who won the R.G. Cox Shield, 1963–64. Left to right: K. Dickinson, J. Richards, K.W. Towells; seated: W. Welsher.

Bicknoller Inn skittles team, early 1960s. Left to right, back row: Jim Henson, David Sully, Jim Walford, Ron Williams, Les Sweetland; front: Bill Sully, Harry Isaac, Donald Langdon.

BICKNOLLER

Bicknoller in the late 1950s.

Bicknoller Parish Church in the 1950s.

Apple pickers in Major Wordsworth's orchard at Bicknoller in the mid-1960s. Left to right, back row: Amy Burnell, Violet Beer, Doreen Woodward, William Lewis, Major Wordsworth, Mrs Sully; sitting: Mary Maine, Arthur Beer.

Major R.G. Wordsworth's cedar wood bungalow (now demolished) which stood near the bus shelter, on the main road, at Bicknoller. Major Wordsworth was in the Indian Army before coming to Bicknoller to start a fruit farm and was said to be a descendant of the famous poet Wordsworth.

Apple pickers at Moorman's Fruit Farm, Bicknoller, 1978. Left to right: Rosemary Newbold, Margaret Sylvester, Heather Bulpin, Joyce Chidgey.

Local MP Ian Liddell-Grainger with his wife Jill and children Sophie, Peter and May. The family reside at Bicknoller.

R.E. (Dick) Greswell pondering over a cup of tea in preparation for Bicknoller's royal Silver Jubilee celebrations, 1977. Mr Greswell had a distinguished career in the Colonial Service, serving in Nigeria for almost 30 years, for which he was made a CMG. During the Second World War he served with the West African Regiment in Burma with the rank of lieutenant-colonel and was awarded the Military Cross. Mr Greswell died in 1979, aged 63.

St John Couch being presented with a silver salver by one of the Bristol University Players, of which he was a former president. The Players made frequent visits to Bicknoller to perform plays in the Village Hall during their tours of the West Country.

Percy Tuckfield, a former landlord of the Bicknoller Inn.

Honey Row Lane, 1962–63.

BICKNOLLER

Trendle Lane, 1962–63.

This stag was born in a field near Bicknoller Moor and stayed there for approximately four years.

Grace Greswell, at the entrance to Wayvile, standing beside an early car in Bicknoller, c.1919.

Richard and Jean Greswell, members of Bicknoller Civil Defence in the 1960s.

Folk dancing at Bicknoller in the 1960s.

Mr George Gadd at the wheel of his solid-tyre Citroën car at Chilcombe, c.1922. Also pictured, left to right are: Mrs Lois Gadd, Marie Gadd, ?, John Gadd.

Mr John Gadd, the local master builder who constructed the school and Clarence House, Bicknoller, amongst other work. He resided at Chilcombe Cottage (now Hilltop) and died in the 1920s.

A group from Bicknoller on a charabanc outing to Gough's Caves, Cheddar, c.1920s. Amongst those pictured are: Hilda Parsons, Dick Canever, Mr Jennings.

Bicknoller and District Scripture Union birthday party, 1930.

A fancy-dress occasion at Bicknoller, c.1910. Amongst those pictured are: Hilda Parsons (Welsh lady), Elsie Parsons, Nancy Gadd, Frederick Canever (man with beard), Winifred Bampton (Scottish lady), Connie Jennings, Gertrude 'Jennie' Jennings.

All dressed up at Bicknoller, c.1910. Left to right: Elsie Parsons, Frederick Canever, Nancy Gadd.

Fancy-dress group at a garden fête at Bicknoller, 1921.

Children's fancy dress at Bicknoller, 1921.

A group at Newton Farm, Bicknoller, c.1920. Left to right: Peggy Thomas, Mabel Taylor, Nina Taylor, Hilda Parsons, ?.

Haymaking at Newton Farm in the late 1920s. Ruby Thomas is patting the horse.

After haymaking at Newton Farm in the late 1920s. Holding the horse is Sidney Thomas.

Peggy Thomas holding the horse at Newton Farm in the late 1920s.

Hilda Parsons with her decorated bicycle at Saffins, Newton, 1921.

The vet's visit to Newton Farm, c.1930s. **Left to right:** *Mr Hall (vet), Elsie Thomas, Alf Chidgey, Sidney Thomas.*

John Thomas at Newton, c.1935.

Three young ladies, c.1912. **Left to right:** *Hilda Parsons, Lilian Tozer, Elsie Parsons.*

Bridesmaids Maud Shutler (left) and Hilda Parsons for the wedding of Elsie Parsons and Sidney Arthur Thomas, 1915.

Wedding guests in the late 1960s. **Left to right:** *Edna Jennings, Mrs Crump, Alice Jennings, Hilda Parsons, Geoffrey Jennings.*

Woolston Grange, which dates from the sixteenth century.

Postmen Joe Millard and William Lewis at Bicknoller in 1947.

Ernie Tarr (chauffeur) and Florence May (later Trickey), employees of Dr and Mrs House, of Bicknoller, c.1932.

'Chocolate box' cottage at Bicknoller.

Bicknoller postman Frederick Canever, c.1910. During the 1920s there were three postmen in the village – Frederick Canever, Alan Fookes and 'Dappy' Slade. 'Junk' mail must have been around even in those days!

William E. Lewis, who had a grocer's and newsagent's shop in Bicknoller and also delivered the mail, c.1950.

BICKNOLLER

Line drawing of Great Hall Croft, Bicknoller, former residence of the late Mr and Mrs H.B. Mayor.

Cliff Trickey preparing a cider cheese in Mrs Jean Greswell's cider house in the 1980s. Cliff was a bricklayer by trade, but also acted as Bicknoller's unofficial barber.

Celebrating Halloween in Bicknoller Village Hall in the 1980s.

Cottage at Chapmans Combe, c.1920.

Preparing for Halloween at the Bicknoller Inn in the 1970s. Glynn Taylor is holding the pumpkin and Cliff Trickey is behind the bar.

Right: *Royal British Legion standard-bearers Frank Hawkins* (left) *and Walter Langdon. Frank was standard-bearer for the Bicknoller branch for 37 years and Walter was a member of the local branch before moving to Williton, where he became standard-bearer. The Bicknoller branch now also incorporates West Quantoxhead, Nettlecombe and Monksilver. On 6 October 1919, Major Yalden Thompson called a meeting of demobilised soldiers and sailors at the Bicknoller schoolroom when it was unanimously decided to form a 'Post of the Comrades of the Great War' and 15 members were enrolled, with Major Thompson as 'Captain'. On 1 July 1921, the 'Comrades of the Great War, Bicknoller Post', was wound up and it was agreed to carry on as a branch of the British Legion (later to become Royal).*

St John Couch and Lyn Dickinson as the Tailor and Simpkin the cat in The Tailor of Gloucester, *performed at Bicknoller Village Hall, 1970.*

St John Couch (left) *and Tom Besley in* The Tailor of Gloucester, *1970.*

Walter Welsher holding a self-made violin, c.1970. Walter served as batman (an attendant serving an officer) to Major R.T. Baxter and also worked for him when they retired from the Army.

Kevin Grant and Martin Clark (holding fox), *1972.*

BICKNOLLER

Christmas card scene at Bicknoller, 1977.

Bakery stall at a morning market in Bicknoller Village Hall, c.1966. Left to right: Audrey Lyddon, Ann Trickey, Ann Tuckfield, Jack Currington.

Icicles at Bicknoller, 1977.

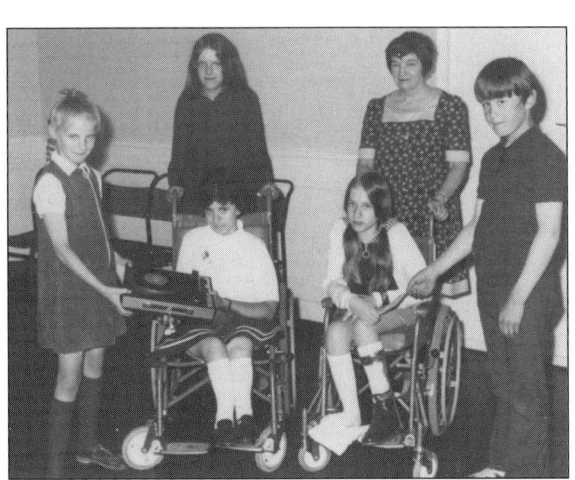

Left: *Bicknoller Youth Club members Melanie Brewer and Andrew Godfrey presenting a record player and gift card to two young disabled residents of Sandhill Park in the 1970s. Money was raised for the gifts by the collection of old newspapers by club members. The Youth Club was formed in 1972 by the Revd Keith Elwood and ran for approximately ten years under the guidance of Jack and Joyce Barber and Sue Rutt. The club met in the barn (now the village shop and Post Office) and played a prominent part in securing a silver cup for the village in the smaller sub-section of the national 'Best Kept Village' competition in 1975. They collected 20 sacks of litter in one evening and really got the village going in a general spruce-up. Bicknoller youths now share joint meetings with Crowcombe Youth Club.*

Bicknoller Village Hall

The first Bicknoller Village Hall committee was formed in 1926 during the incumbency of the late Revd A.E. Couch, whose son, Mr E. Llewellyn St John Couch, was chairman of the hall committee (which went by the name Moor-by-the-Green) at the time of its official opening. After the project had been mooted in 1926 the years were not particularly fruitful; money came in, but the goal could hardly be seen through a telescope.

The 1920s and '30s came and went and then the war drove the project into the background. Almost immediately afterwards Bicknoller launched a full-scale offensive, and the first day of triumph came in 1954 when Mrs H.B. Mayor laid the foundation-stone of the new hall. Later that year the long-awaited hall was in use after much fund-raising, hard work and planning. Notable among the fund-raising was the effort by the children of the village in 1954 when they ran an entire fête and raised £54.

The hall's formal opening was on 26 June 1955, when all its furnishings had been completed. It was officially opened by Mr George C. Wyndham, of Orchard Wyndham, Williton, in the presence of many parishioners.

Mr Couch, who presided, had the support of a platform that included Mrs H.B. Mayor as guest of honour (her husband, the late Mr Henry Bickersteth Mayor, having bequeathed to the village the land known as Moor-by-the-Green on which the hall is

Bicknoller Village Hall, which opened in 1954.

built), Miss Gertrude ('Jennie') Jennings, Mr Wyndham, Mrs J.W. Barber (vice-chairman of the committee), Major R.T. Baxter (treasurer), and the five trustees of the hall, the Revd W.S. Thomas, Mr W.T. James, Mrs A.N. Capewell, Mrs R.E. Harenc and Mr E.A. Greswell, together with the following committee members: Mr Currington, Mrs Dinwiddy, Mr P. Maine, Mr L. Gimblett, Miss Melhuish, Mr C.A. Anderson, Mrs Burnell, Mrs Fritz and the Revd H.A. Dunn (vicar).

In an amusing speech, Miss Gertrude ('Jennie') Jennings, 'as one whose home has always been at Bicknoller, yet who is also a part-time resident of Williton', thanked Mr Wyndham for his services. 'It is a joy to have this hall', continued Miss Jennings.

So many of us have loved the old schoolroom, with its happy memories and its ghastly inconveniences, and

Gertrude ('Jennie') Jennings speaking at the official opening of Bicknoller Village Hall, 1955. Left to right: Sallyann Bowerman (who presented Mrs Mayor with a bouquet), Miss Gertrude ('Jennie') Jennings, Mr G.C. Wyndham, Mrs H.B. Mayor, Mrs A.N. Capewell, Mrs Fritz, Mr E. Ll. St John Couch, Mr A.E. Greswell (hidden), Major R.T. Baxter, Mrs J.W. Barber, ?.

A licensed lay reader, he held the Bishop's authority to preach in any church in the diocese.

St John Couch was at one time the £5-a-year clerk of Stogumber Parish Council, but at Bicknoller he was chairman, holding this office from 1949–73. He was a fearless champion of local causes – and greatly respected in clashes with higher authority. He also became chairman of Bicknoller and District branch of the Royal British Legion, and the village Flower Show was among organisations which could count on his interest and help. He was also prominent in the Friends of Quantock organisation and had been its chairman.

Many Bicknoller folk would say that there is a monument to St John Couch. This is the splendid Village Hall, which reached its half-century in 2004. He was the driving force behind the hall's construction (first mooted in 1926), following the Second World War. He was the chairman of the curiously named Moor-by-the-Green committee.

Keen on drama, St John Couch had trodden the boards many times. He was with the former Nettlecombe Players under the watchful eye of playwright Phoebe Rees and, on his home ground, was producer as well as player. He appeared in numerous plays and sketches, and would turn his nimble mind and penchant for wit into writing skits and drolleries which could raise the roof. St John Couch was also a former president of Bristol University Players and would arrange for them to visit the village whilst on tour to perform plays. Steeped in parish history, both of Bicknoller and Stogumber, he collaborated with his uncle, the late Revd E.A. Couch, in the production of noteworthy pageantry.

St John Couch married, in 1939, Miss Joan Kershaw of Bicknoller.

Gertrude Mary Jennings

Miss Gertrude Mary ('Jennie') Jennings, formerly of Clarence House, Bicknoller, was born at Devonport but grew up in Bicknoller and came from a family that had lived there for several generations. Her great-great-grandfather had moved to Bicknoller from Stogumber with his family in about 1815. She chose a career in nursing and trained at the Royal Devon and Exeter Hospital, where she gained the gold medal for being the best of her year in 1922. In the 1920s and '30s she worked in London as a midwife at the Royal Lying-in Hospital in York Road, just south of the Thames. She recalled going to deliver babies in the dreadful slums in the area, but thought that the people were wonderful. She became a sister-tutor in midwifery and remembered that Queen Mary, who was patron of the hospital, would come into her lectures and listen at the back. The Queen asked her to take no notice of her and just carry on as usual. She joined Queen Alexandra's

Gertrude ('Jennie') (left) and Constance Jennings taking tea at Bicknoller, c.1907.

Constance Dinwiddy (left), Gertrude 'Jennie' Jennings and Richard Dinwiddy at Bicknoller, c.1950.

Royal Army Nursing Corps during the Second World War and was principal matron of a hospital in India with the rank of colonel.

'Jennie' returned to Bicknoller shortly after the war to look after her mother and when she died became sister at Williton Hospital, a position she held with much respect and esteem until her retirement. Even the most inclement weather did not deter her from her duties at Williton, walking the three miles to the hospital when heavy snowfalls blocked the roads to traffic.

One of her many interests in Bicknoller was the Women's Institute, of which she was a founder, committee member and a past president. She knew and remembered all the members' birthdays and would telephone each one to wish them a happy birthday. In 1965 she represented Bicknoller WI at a garden party at Buckingham Palace.

Also featuring prominently in her life was the Parish Church where she was organist for many years. She was also a past president of the Bicknoller branch of the Royal British Legion, and was keenly interested in the procurement of the local Village Hall. In addition to her work, she enjoyed classical music and would talk of going to the Royal Opera House before the war. 'Jennie' also greatly enjoyed watching Somerset County Cricket Club.

Sister Jennings was Bicknoller's honorary 'district nurse' and was much loved. She died in April 1986, aged 86.

Growing up in Bicknoller

The following is an account by Mrs Audrey Chawner (neé Lyddon) of the years she spent in Bicknoller:

I arrived in Bicknoller in 1951 at the age of two months when I was adopted by Spencer and Alice Lyddon, who had lived in the village since the First World War. Even my new grandparents also lived in the village, firstly at Wayvile House then at the bottom of the village near the Taunton–Minehead road, but both died shortly after moving there. My new home was at The Laurels in Church Lane.

I was baptised at St George's Church in the village, and was also confirmed there and sang in the church choir. In older days my mother helped with the Sunday school, which I enjoyed very much and looked forward to Sundays. I also loved music, later learning to play the piano.

When I was five years old I attended primary school at Williton, and when 11 I went to Williton Secondary Modern School. My parents had attended the old school in the village, which later became a Post Office, being run by Mrs G. Spark. Just across the road was a little village shop run by Mrs G. Lewis. It was a lovely little shop in those days where you could go and spend your old 1d. on penny chews and sherbert dips, also tea and biscuits and things needed for the home. You could also get your daily newspaper there.

In those days there was very little to do in the evenings. There was a Village Hall used for whist drives, Parish Council meetings, plays, morning markets and Mr St John Couch's evenings for the whole family in dancing and entertainment. There was a Mothers' Union branch to which my mother belonged. Our vicars at the time were the Revds Dunn and Legg, followed by the Revds Simpson and Scammell. Mr Couch helped when it was Holy Communion and for other services in the church.

In 1958 the first Bicknoller Flower Show was held in the Village Hall and committee room. The show is still going, being held in July every year and much looked forward to. Bingo was held every other Saturday evening in the hall, run by the late Sid Bryant. People came from surrounding villages and it was a good night with refreshments and excellent prizes. The Christmas bingo was the best with all the festive prizes you could think of.

As the years went on there were a number of houses and bungalows built in the village. The only other place you could go at dinner times and evenings was the local village pub – the Bicknoller Inn. In the old days it was run by Mr and Mrs T. Rowlands, then by Mr and Mrs P. Tuckfield. The local Hunts met at the pub during the hunting season before making their way up the road and onto the Quantock Hills.

Then the Taunton–Minehead road was modernised and called the A358. I can remember when I was at school we had very bad snow – you could walk on top of it up the road to the church. Later there was another change in the village – the old Post Office closed and there was a new one run by Mrs R. Cartwright after she had an addition built at the side of her house. Now there is a Post Office and shop in the transformed barn adjoining the Village Hall.

All the roads in the village now have names such as Trendle Lane, Honeyrow Lane, Church Lane and many more. We were even given postcodes by the Royal Mail to add to our addresses. The Village Hall was now being used by more organisations and for further events – Women's Institute, Quantock Wives, jumble sales, morning markets and for plays performed by villagers. Apples could even be bought at the side of the main road from Major Wordsworth's orchards. Later on you could go just a few yards up the road and buy tomatoes from Mr and Mrs Moorman, the parents of John Moorman, who has now passed away. When he was living in the village he had fields at the top of Honeyrow Lane and grew blackcurrants, raspberries and, later, apples. His wife Margaret ran a catering business for parties and weddings. She was a very popular person, and her father, Maurice Wilson, was secretary of Bicknoller Flower Show for a good number of years. As the month of July approached I would go to Mr Wilson for some Bicknoller Flower Show draw books and I would always sell the most. During that time, Starkey, Knight & Ford, who were a brewery which supplied some of the local pubs, gave two large marquees to Bicknoller Flower Show, and after all the years of wear and tear they still have them.

When I come home to Somerset and go through the village I notice the changes that have occurred since I lived and grew up in Bicknoller. I do have some very happy memories of all the time that I spent there. At the moment I am living up North in a village called Ramsbottom, about 12 miles from the city of Manchester.

Well, I think I have told you all about my life in Bicknoller. I do hope that the people living in the village at present spend the rest of their time there as happy as I was. Best wishes and good luck to you all.

Audrey Lyddon at the time of her confirmation in 1962.

Royal Occasions

Bicknoller celebrates Queen Victoria's Diamond Jubilee in 1897. Among those pictured are: John Escott, George Parsons (Dashwoods), John Slade, Mrs E. Milton and family, Mrs Walter Slade, Mrs Taylor (late of the New Inn), Tilt Cogan, E. Parsons (Newton) and John Edwards (fought in the Crimean War).

Bicknoller celebrates Queen Victoria's Golden Jubilee in 1887.

Mr Slade (landlord) with family and friends celebrating Queen Victoria's Golden Jubilee outside the New Inn (now the Bicknoller Inn).

A decorated wagon and shire horses on Great Moor in celebration of Queen Victoria's Golden Jubilee in 1887. The carters were: Jesse Carrott, John Langdon, Edwin Dibble, Joseph Parsons, William Ash, William Gore, Charlie Burge, Ephraim Grandfield, James Grandfield, John Escott. The horse owners were G.H. Parsons, L. Lethbridge, C. Weetch and C. Parsons.

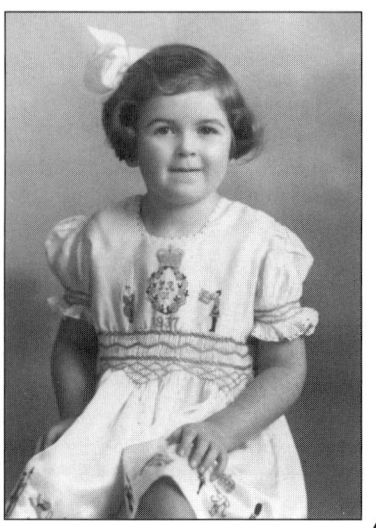

Ann Rutt wearing the dress made by her mother to commemorate the Coronation of King George VI in 1937.

Coronation Celebrations, 1953

Bicknoller's Coronation Day, on Tuesday 2 June 1953, was honoured in the best country tradition, with everyone joining in the church services and fun to celebrate the crowning of Queen Elizabeth II. The bells pealed and the village was gay with bunting and floral decorations. Mr M. Carrott captained the bell-ringers.

The main stage for the celebrations was the large field adjoining the church, which Mr Gimblett lent for the purpose. Here, on a well-prepared track, sports for children and adults provided much amusement and, in many cases, unaccustomed exercise. Mrs Dunn and Mrs Polgrahan supervised. Tea was bountifully served to all by Mrs J. Barber and her competent band of helpers in the schoolroom, which had been suitably decorated by Mrs P. Maine. Before sitting down to tea, all the children were handed souvenir mugs by Mrs G.H. Billings, who qualified for this task of honour as the parishioner having most years to her credit. Two of her close rivals, Mrs T. Morrison and Mrs Lucraft, presented prizes to the winners in the children's and adults' sports respectively. Later, ices were served to the children in the Vicarage garden, and Messrs S. Lyddon and P. Maine were in charge of free skittling for ladies' and gentlemen's prizes.

In the evening the schoolroom was packed for dancing, conducted by Messrs R. and M. Rutt and Mrs M. Bishop, and when dusk came a large crowd of young and old gathered around a huge bonfire in Mr Gimblett's field. Refreshments were handed round, and the finest display of fireworks ever seen in the village was ably handled by Messrs J. Barber and Currington. The day closed with the joining of hands round the fire for the singing of 'Auld Lang Syne', and as the happy crowd made its way homewards remarks of enjoyment and appreciation were heard on all sides.

The whole programme was planned and, with the aid of many volunteers, carried through by a committee consisting of the vicar, the Revd H.A. Dunn (chairman), Mesdames J. Barber, H. Burnell, C. Dinwiddy, ? Dunn and P. Maine, Group Captain Farrington, Mr C.A. Anderson, Miss M. Melhuish and Mrs. N. Bishop.

The Queen's Silver Jubilee hat competition, 1977. Left to right: *Mrs Pritchard, ?, Mrs Thompson, Mrs Sentance-Smith, Miss G. Jennings, Miss O. Davis.*

Gertrude ('Jennie') Jennings about to unveil the wrought-iron gates erected at the pathway to the Village Hall to commemorate Queen Elizabeth II's Silver Jubilee in 1977.

Village gathering to celebrate Queen Elizabeth II's Silver Jubilee, 1977.

Alison Maddock as 'Daisy Daisy' for Queen Elizabeth II's Silver Jubilee celebrations in 1977.

Christopher Rutt as 'Silver Shred' as part of Queen Elizabeth II's Silver Jubilee celebrations in 1977.

Bicknoller girls' cricket team, 1977. Left to right, back row: Julie Cummings, ?, Sallyann Johnson, Elizabeth Lewis, Charlotte Darke, Suzanne Hole, ?; front: Helen and Christine Moorman, Mandy Baker, Alison Maddock.

Bicknoller boys' cricket team, 1977. Left to right, back row: Major R. Northcott-Green, P. Sweetland, D. Maddock, D. Rutt, A. Godfrey, A. Trickett, D. Spence, K. Grant, M. Hole, J. Barber; front: S. Baker, D. Maddock, C. Rutt.

Bicknoller celebrating the Golden Jubilee of Queen Elizabeth II in 2002.

Extracts from Bicknoller CE School Logbook, 1881–1900

The following extracts make fascinating reading and reflect wider social changes. No names have been mentioned here where embarrassment might be caused and only initials have been inserted in certain places. The school was closed in 1911, but there are no logbook entries available after 1900. The logbook is kept at the Somerset Record Office at Taunton.

1881

3 Jan: Reopened school after having sat at the Christmas examinations held at Bristol, 1880 – Margaret Lewis Rodger.

18 Jan: Tuesday morning, only 19 present – snowstorm.

31 Jan: Re-commenced work – school has been closed since the 18th because of bad weather.

25 Feb: Children not so punctual as they should be.

18 March: Mrs Wood took sewing class. Children very troublesome during singing lesson – had to make them sit still for 10 minutes to get discipline.

25 May: The school was examined today by the Revd W. Mitchell, Diocesan Inspector.

13 June: Children had holiday as it is their Club Day.

1 July: Attendance has been bad this week through the prevalence of water-pox.

29 July: Marked progress in the reading of the upper standards.

5 Aug: Sewing taken by Ladies' Committee. School closed for four weeks for harvest holidays.

5 Sept: Reopened school – small attendance as gleaning is not finished.

8 Oct: Children not so regular this week as parents have been lifting their potatoes.

25 Nov: Several children sent home because of sickness. Wet weather has lowered attendance.

1882

13 Jan: Attendance better, children more diligent.

24 Jan: This afternoon, after our regular work, the children received their prizes and read some poetry. Our vicar, the Revd W.B. Wood, presented them with a few remarks. The children were very pleased.

17 March: First standard had a blackboard arithmetic lesson instead of an object lesson. The I standard arithmetic and III standard geography is far from satisfactory.

28 April: Registers not marked as school was examined by the Diocesan Inspector. Forty-three children present, also Mrs Wood.

5 May: I and III standards are still not as well up as they should be.

24 May: Copy of the Revd W.W. Herringham's report: 'The tone and discipline good. The infants gave evidence of having been carefully taught. Groups I and II, comprising of Standards I, II and III, were rather deficient in their knowledge of Holy Scripture, the answers coming from only a few. The elder children answered well.'

The school, Bicknoller, c.1900. After its closure it became a Post Office and also the venue for social events; Mr Spark had a workshop on the site. It is now a private residence.

BICKNOLLER

10 July:	Summary of Inspector's report: 'In some respects fair results have been produced, but the First Standard is particularly weak and arithmetic throughout the school is unsatisfactory. The infants need extra attention. Miss Rodgers will shortly receive her certificate.
21 July:	Attendance bad – whortleberry picking.
2 Sept:	Frances Jane Symes entered upon her duties as monitor at 1s. [5p] a week.
27 Oct:	Poor attendance through the bad weather. Only seven children on Tuesday – roads being impassable.
22 Dec:	Better attendance than previous two weeks. School upset by unruly boy. Miss Margaret Lewis Rodgers resigned.

1883
15 Jan:	Miss Kate Llewellin started duties as school mistress.
19 Jan:	Children have been in good time, worked well but too noisy when changing.
26 Jan:	I and II Standards backward in arithmetic. Some new desks were placed in school and three old ones removed.
2 Feb:	Attendance not been so good owing to very stormy weather.
6 April:	Very poor attendance this week, so many of the little ones are suffering with whooping cough.
13 April:	Was forced to punish a boy for disobedience. Average attendance for week, 40.
6 June:	Mr Thorne visited this afternoon – two parents have been summoned for the irregular attendance of their children.
8 Aug:	Inspector's report: 'The 1st Standard is a very weak one in all respects and arithmetic is taught with slight success throughout the school. In other respects the children have done fairly well. Discipline is satisfactory...'
20 Sept:	Found slight improvement in writing and spelling. Began giving home lessons this week.
2 Nov:	Children have been more punctual and home lessons have been fairly well done throughout the week. The 1st and 2nd Standards seem to have improved slightly in writing and spelling.

1884
7 Jan:	Harriet Burge took the place of J. Symes as monitress.
25 Jan:	Attendance rather small owing to bad weather. I have withdrawn the names of four children from the register – two Chidzeys and two Bakers.
13 Feb:	Poor attendance – weather wet and cold. Two children sent home because they had ringworm and two others have bad heads.
30 May:	Good attendance all week except Thursday when several of the children went to Stogumber, it being Club Day there.
15 Sept:	School closed again from the 15th to the 26th owing to the spread of scarlet fever.
13 Oct:	Louisa Dibble took the place of Harriet Burge as monitress.

1887
15 March:	A very heavy fall of snow today – no school in consequence on Wednesday. Only a few children present all week.
13 July:	Holiday was given today as the Jubilee festivities took place here. The next two days very wet.
29 July:	Attendance poor – many children went to Minehead races on the 26th and Crowcombe Jubilee celebrations on the 28th.
12 Aug:	Many children away gleaning.
7 Oct:	Infants are very pleased with the Kindergarten gifts.

1888
17 Feb:	Weather has been very severe this week. On Thursday school did not open owing to a heavy fall of snow.
29 June:	Annie Grandfield replaced Louisa Dibble as monitress.
18 July:	Mrs Wood invited this morning for musical drill. Mr Thorne also visited this afternoon. No better attendance. Have taught Standard III compound multiplication and addition of fractions to Standard V.
17 Sept:	School reopened – very few children present owing to late harvest, the children away gleaning.

1889
29 Nov:	Two children are very irregular in attendance and are most backward in lessons.

1890
6 Jan:	School reopened. Admitted three fresh children.
3 April:	Much better attendance. Standards II and III girls are the weakest in arithmetic.
19 Dec:	There was a very small school today, only 15 children present owing to snow. Revd W.B. Wood visited and gave the prizes to those present; the other prizes were given in the evening at the children's entertainment.

1891
13 March:	No school after the 9th owing to the heavy snow.
20 March:	Rather a poor attendance this week, some children being unable to get to school as the lanes were blocked with snow.
17 July:	Attendance not so good this week – some of the elder children helping in the hayfields.
5 Aug:	Holiday given today – the children had a school feast at the Vicarage.
16 Nov:	Received a new set of reading books for Standard II and some drawing books for the Infants.

1892
18 Jan:	The school bank was opened this morning with 11 depositors.
25 Jan:	Six other children have become depositors in the bank.
11 Feb:	A half-holiday given this afternoon owing to a confirmation held in this Parish Church.

19 Feb:	No children were able to get to school today due to snow.
27 March:	The Hon. Mrs and Miss Trefusis visited this morning, 39 children present.
28 April:	Alice Grandfield took the place of Annie Grandfield as monitress.
19 Sept:	Opened school after five weeks' holiday, only 26 present – some kept away through measles.
14 Oct:	Very wet week and especially so this morning, only 14 children were present.

1893

16 Jan:	Miss Mabel Ebdon entered the school as mistress. Several children away with whooping cough.
15 Feb:	Children went to church this morning, it being Ash Wednesday.
16 Feb:	Writing on slates instead of copy book this morning for the higher standards.
20 Feb:	Willie Escott came to school after the registers were called.
6 April:	Readmitted Florence Dibble this morning.
1 May:	Harry and Florence Dibble came too late this afternoon for them to be entered on the register.
6 July:	School closed for Royal Wedding day.
20 Nov:	Writing in all classes seems to have been much improved lately. Infants very backward in arithmetic.
27 Nov:	Average for week, 27. The penny bank is in a flourishing condition.

1894

22 Jan:	Messrs Fry & Son presented the school with some very valuable specimens of cocoa, chocolate, etc for use in object lessons.
19 Feb:	Readmitted Albert Carrott.
2 April:	Readmitted Arthur Kilgour and admitted Violet Kilgour, Albert Peppin and Clara Peppin.
13 April:	A boy was sent home this afternoon for impertinence.
16 April:	Admitted Beatrice Peppin.
14 June:	I have decided to mark the early children in red ink and those late in black.
19 June:	Have re-classified children this morning for next year's work. Admitted Lucy Hall.
26 June:	Admitted Florence, Frederick and Minnie Jones today. Albert Carrott, Annie Welsher and Albert Peppin have left since the examination.
5 Nov:	Average for the past week, 25. Admitted two children, Edna and Nellie Howe.

1895

10 July:	Lydia Hawkins, Mabel Barker, Clare Peppin, Walter Williams, Rosie and Freddie Hawkins lost their marks through going whortleberry picking in the dinner hour.
17 July:	Children improving in arithmetic throughout the school.
2 Sept:	Average for past week 31, a slight improvement.
13 Nov:	Three children are suffering from scarletina.

1896

7 Jan:	Admitted John Binding to Standard 4.
10 Jan:	Average for past week, 27. G. Ebdon has this past week joined Prof. Cusack's correspondence classes for scholarship course.
30 Jan:	We took tables this afternoon instead of mental arithmetic.
19 March:	History still is rather weak in the higher group.
23 March:	Admitted Sarah, Joseph and Ernest Sully.
28 May:	Miss Ada Hoskins commenced as school mistress; Mabel Barker as monitress.
22 June:	John Binding has left the school, his father is a sailor and he has returned to Watchet. Word building was not well done today, but other lessons were fair.
14 July:	Revd W.B. Wood brought 12 history books. Harry and Florence Dibble absent this morning; the boy goes to Thorncombe once a week, the residence of one of the managers, consequently losing attendances.
20 July:	Admitted four children from Woolston Moor who can neither read nor write. They are gypsies and only one has ever been inside a school before.
3 Aug:	Small attendance, several out gleaning.
14 Sept:	Reopened and several absent this morning. The four gypsy children have left the district. Bertha Grandfield is now monitress instead of Mabel Barker, who wishes to continue lessons in school with the upper division.
18 Sept:	The gypsies have returned to Woolston Moor and the children returned to school.
7 Oct:	The highest attendance to 25 September have been made by Elsie Parsons and Martin Carrott. The highest number of marks for arithmetic have been gained by Ellen Hawkins in Stage I and Walter Carrott in Stage II. The attendances were 117 each.
16 Oct:	Some children have been absent this week picking potatoes and others on account of heavy rain, but work has been fairly done by those present. Elsie Parsons was very unwell.
30 Nov:	Admitted two girls today – Rosie Miles from Watchet and Mabel Hembrow from a private school in Stogumber.
10 Dec:	Ellen Hawkins has been ordered to lie in bed a week by Dr Killick and as mother is ill her sister Lydia is absent too looking after them.
21 Dec:	Ellen Hawkins is better and allowed to return to school.

1897

11 Jan:	Reopened school, small attendance. The medical officer of health called to say that Joseph Sully has scarlet fever and that he has forbidden any other children in the family to come to school for six weeks.
23 March:	Revd W.B. Wood gave Scripture lesson to the Upper Division; several absent picking shellfish.
2 April:	Snowstorm yesterday, only three came in the morning.
10 May:	Three boys who have scarlet fever in their homes come to school. I had to send them home.
21 May:	One little girl who has been in school a short time has gone into the Union with her mother. Two have been away all week at Bristol and four have been absent on account of fevers.

BICKNOLLER

14 June:	Admitted James Welsher, an infant.
21 June:	Closed school for a week in order to celebrate Her Majesty's Diamond Jubilee and record a reign of 60 years.
28 June:	Reopened, a good attendance. Admitted Gladys Mary Chick, six years old.
2 July:	Several absent this afternoon, picking whortleberries.
12 July:	Arithmetic improving, writing not well done, knitting and sewing fair, infants moderate.
30 July:	Work fairly well done by those present all the week, but there are still several away with their parents on the hills picking whortleberries.
20 Sept:	Mrs Murphy took charge of the school; Bertha Grandfield monitress.
24 Sept:	Children in Stage II are much more intelligent and have much better knowledge of their work than those in Stage I, where the younger children are particularly weak.
28 Sept:	Had to insist on the Upper School sitting still for half an hour this morning on account of the repeated disobedience; also had to punish Henry Dibble for his deliberate disobedience.
8 Oct:	The children have been more orderly and work has progressed much better, but the Stage I lower are very backward and dull. Joseph and Ernest Sully have only made two attendances each this week, the other two Sullys and Nellie Hill have not attended since school reopened on 13 September.
15 Oct:	Monthly examination: Stage II have done very well, but Stage I and infants are sadly lacking in intelligence. Edward Hawkins is much in advance of his class, though not fit for Stage I. The two Sully boys have attended much better this week.
26 Nov:	Gave Bertha Grandfield permission for the day off as she is being confirmed this afternoon. Sidney Berryman, who was re-admitted on 25 October, has been absent for the past three weeks and neither of the two Sully girls have attended this quarter.

1898

12 Jan:	A grant of £9 has been made for the purpose of increasing the efficiency of the school and satisfying the demands of the Education Department. Miss Louisa Emily Gouldsmith took charge of school.
18 Feb:	Bertha Grandfield (monitress) absent all week with influenza; Elsie Parsons filled her place.
22 Feb:	Only one child this morning and two in the afternoon, so closed school due to heavy snowfall.
4 July:	Hilda Parsons is away staying at Crowcombe. Harry Dibble in Standard II has been absent since 20 June as he is working for a farmer. Harry Dibble has been granted a Labour Certificate by HM inspector and I have removed his name from the register.
22 July:	Punished P.N. severely for striking the monitor with his fist.
1 Oct:	Mrs Susannah Dymond Harwood took charge of school.
3 Oct:	Admitted Charles Henry Harwood and Alfred Ernest Howard; Lily Lee monitress.

1899

9 Feb:	Mr Frank Adkins, from the United Kingdom Band of Hope Union, gave a temperance lecture this morning.
28 April:	Ernest Sully was brought in at 1.45 by his sister, having been playing truant all morning.
5 May:	Admitted one new scholar, aged 12 – very backward, does not know all her letters.
29 May:	Admitted Daniel and Nellie McCarthy from Quantock Moor.
10 July:	Admitted fresh scholar this morning – Robert Sully, aged two years 10 months.
11 Sept:	Reopened school after five weeks' harvest holiday – attendance poor. Lily Lee (late monitress) has left and Ellen Hawkins taken her place.
12 Sept:	Aid grant of £5 for the increase of the salary of the head teacher.
18 Sept:	A very wet morning. Ellen, Edward and Freddie Hawkins came after 10a.m. so lost their marks. Mary Siderfin commenced her duties as monitress.
1 Dec:	First visit of inspector under ART. 84/G: 'The majority of the desks now in use are unfit and should be replaced by more modern ones. The children are neat and well behaved.' – Alfred H. Lacey.

1900

23 Jan:	I have taken spelling today instead of copy books as the children are backward in spelling.
2 Feb:	Revd Wood took Upper Division for Scripture. There was such a severe snowstorm on Friday we had no school.
9 Feb:	Revd Wood called Wednesday to tell us the new desks were ordered.
16 Feb:	No school, severe snow on Wednesday and rain on Thursday. Only four children came each day and they were so wet I was obliged to send them home.
20 Feb:	New desks arrived. Small school on account of heavy rain.
10 May:	Second visit of inspector under ART 84/G: 'Mrs Harwood has got her school into capital condition, the order, neatness and general conditions being highly satisfactory. The new desks are a great improvement.' – Alfred H. Lacey.
24 Aug:	Ascension Day and Her Majesty's birthday. Registers were marked at nine to enable us to go to church and a half-day holiday was given in the afternoon.

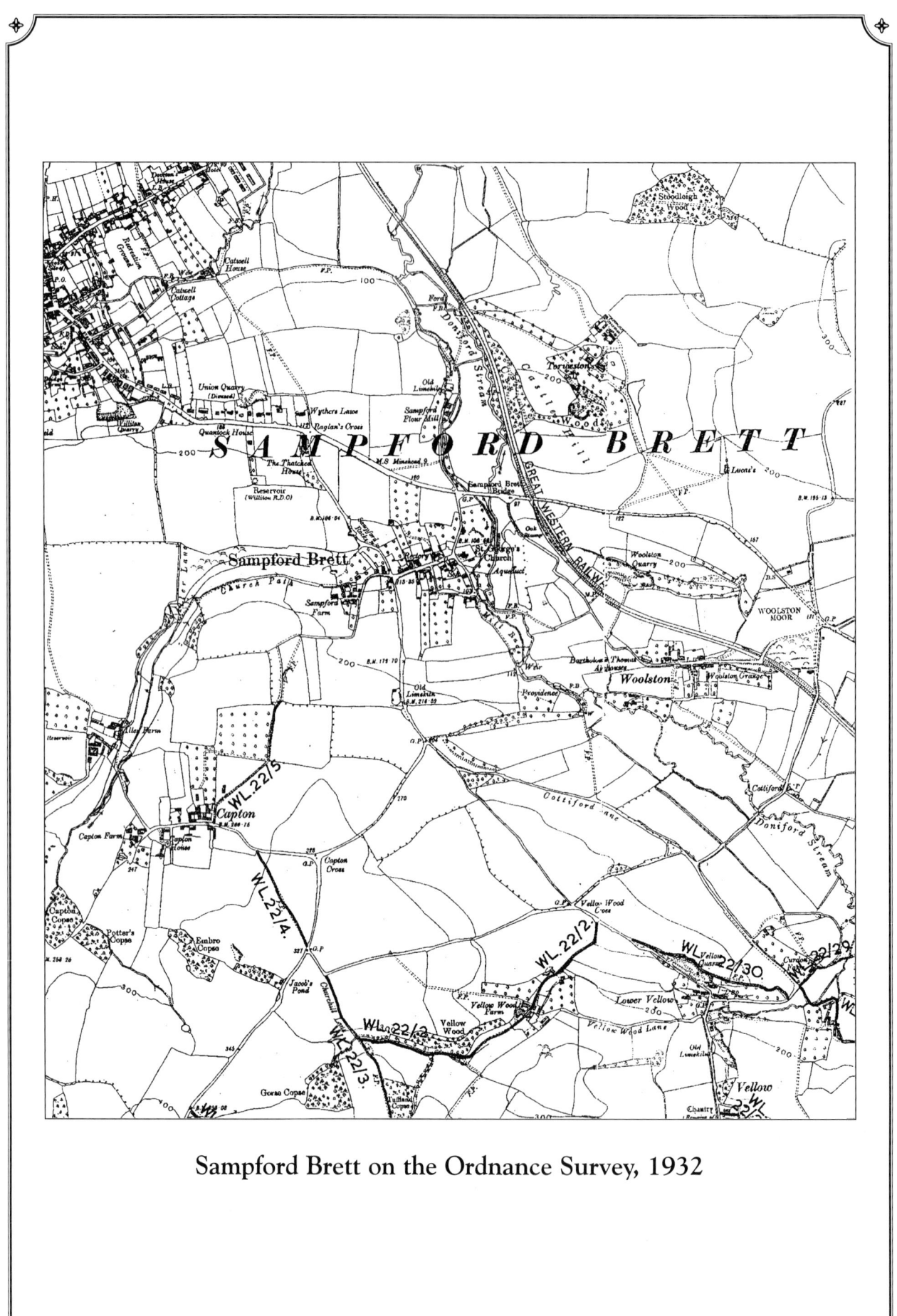

Sampford Brett on the Ordnance Survey, 1932

Chapter 3
Sampford Brett

The parish of Sampford Brett takes its name from a sandy ford which crossed the Doniford stream and from the Brett family. Torweston, sheltering under Castle Hill, lies east of the stream, and Aller Farm is situated south-west of Sampford village. At the end of the eighteenth century the main road through the parish, crossing the village street at its western end, was part of a route between Williton and Stogumber. This route was later cut by the road from Tower Hill to Bicknoller, and in 1807 became part of a new turnpike route from Williton to Taunton. A railway line was cut through the parish from the foot of Castle Hill when the West Somerset Railway opened in 1862. From 1930 onwards houses have been built beside the main road north of the village in the development of Tower Hill and also at Catwell. The petrol service station on the A358 was also a 1930s addition, but was closed for the duration of the Second World War. The Brett Close and Croft Meadow village building developments took place in the 1960s and '70s.

The village lies about a mile south of Williton between the Quantock and Brendon Hills in a shallow valley formed by the Sampford stream running from Aller Farm. Its single main street, widened in 1891, has St George's Church at its eastern end. Although the village has now lost its school, Post Office and shop, it is still a lively community with the church and Village Hall being the focal points of communal and social life. The parish population over the last 50 years has been 221 in 1951, 291 in 1971 and 280 in 2002.

Sampford manor was held by Alnod in 1066 and by Hugh d'Avranches, Earl of Chester, with William as his under-tenant in 1086. Torweston manor was held in 1066 by Lefsin, and in 1086 by William de Mohun with Hugh as under-tenant. Sampford manor was recorded in the Domesday Book in 1086. The over-lordship remained as part of the Mohuns' honour of Dunster until 1777 or later. Of that honour Simon Brito or Brett, from whose family the parish gained its distinguishing name, held two knights' fees, possibly both Sampford and Torweston, in the twelfth century. In 1170 Sir Simon's eldest son, Sir Richard de Brett, was one of the four knights who murdered Thomas á Beckett in Canterbury Cathedral. Another of the murderers was Sir Reginald Fitz-Urse, of neighbouring Williton. After the murder the four knights were sent on a penitential crusade to the Holy Land by the Pope, but all died within five years and were buried in Jerusalem.

Sir William de Brett held both Sampford and Torweston in 1280; he died in 1295 and his tomb is in the vestry of St George's Church. His heir was his

Looking west up the main street at Sampford Brett, c.1930. Note the oil-lamp on the left.

Aerial view of Sampford Brett, 1993.

son Adam, who in 1306 was granted a weekly market in Sampford on Mondays with a yearly fair there for three days at the feast of St George (23 April). Adam Brett had a licence in 1316 to crenellate his dwelling at Torweston, thus giving it the appearance of a castle. This probably gave rise to the field names North and South Castle and Castle Copse on the slopes of Castle Hill.

The Bretts continued in possession until 1359, when they sold the two manors and the dower lands to Hugh Courtenay, Earl of Devon, and his wife Margaret. The manors of Sampford Brett and Torweston remained in the possession of the Courtenays for nearly 500 years. The widow of the last John Courtenay, Margaret, held the estate until her death in 1743. Being childless, it passed to John's sister, Elizabeth, wife of John Chichester, of Arlington, Devon. Elizabeth died in 1763, leaving the manors to her granddaughter, Anna Maria Paston, wife of George Throckmorton, of Coughton, Warwickshire. Margaret Courtenay was a descendant of the Wyndham family, of Orchard Wyndham, and she presented to St George's Church a silver paten and alms dish which bear her coat of arms. The coat of arms is also depicted in the west window of the church; the original window was destroyed by the blast from a land mine dropped from a German aeroplane in 1940.

The estate descended in the Courtenay family until 1846 when Robert George Throckmorton, of Buckland, Berkshire, sold it to Sir Peregrine Periam Fuller Palmer Acland, Bt, who owned the St Audries and Fairfield estates. He was the founder and first chairman of the West Somerset Railway. When Sir Peregrine's daughter, Isabel Harriet, married Sir Alexander Hood, Bt, MP, in 1849 the Sampford estate was settled on her. They took the joint name of Acland-Hood and lived at St Audries and Fairfield estates. Isabel had married at the age of 18 and bore nine children. Sir Alexander was a member of the well-known Hood naval family, many of whom were admirals, and the battleship HMS *Hood*, sunk during the Second World War, was named after one of them. He was Member of Parliament for West Somerset from 1859–68 and died in 1892. His eldest son, Sir Alexander

Sir Peregrine Periam Fuller Palmer Acland, Bt (1789–1871).

Sir Alexander Acland-Hood, Bt, (1819–92).

Dame Isabel Harriet Fuller Acland-Hood (1832–1903).

Sir Alexander Acland-Hood, Bt, the first Lord St Audries, d.1917.

Peregrine, the second and last Lord St Audries, d.1971.

Fuller Acland-Hood, was the fourth Baronet of St Audries in Somerset and sixth Baronet of Hartington in Derbyshire. He was Member of Parliament for West Somerset from 1892–1911, when he was elevated to the peerage, becoming Baron St Audries; he died in 1917. During his Parliamentary career he became Vice-Chamberlain in 1900, Chief Whip of the Conservative and Unionist Party in 1902 under Mr Balfour and a Privy Councillor in 1904. His elder son, Peregrine, the second and last Lord St Audries, was forced by taxation to sell the Sampford estate to William Wyndham and Sir Walter Trevelyan between 1924 and 1931, but the lordship of the manors was not included in the sale. Lord St Audries, a bachelor, died in 1971 at the age of 77. Among his attributes, Peregrine was an accomplished organist. As he died without issue, his niece, Lady Elizabeth Periam Gass, eldest daughter of the Hon. John Acland-Hood, the last Lord St Audries's younger brother, who died in 1964, inherited. At the time of writing, Lady Gass, widow of Sir Michael Gass, KCMG, resides at Fairfield, Stogursey, and became Her Majesty's Lord Lieutenant of Somerset in 2000.

Torweston Farm, c.1900. The farmhouse is said to be erected on the residual foundations of the old castle.

In the mid-eighteenth century Torweston Barton was the name given to the farmhouse which stood in the garden of the present Torweston Farm, a large late-nineteenth century house with a two-storeyed cider house, office, coach-house and stables beyond. On lower ground to the north is an extensive group of contemporary farm buildings; a mill still stands in the central range. In 1851 the Corner brothers farmed the 435 acres of Torweston, employing 30 men, women and boys, as well as two household servants, and in 1869 the lessee supplemented his workers' wages with turnips and straw. The West Somerset Yeomanry used a large field on Torweston Farm in 1906 as a camp-site for training; some 450 men, with their mounts, camped there for 17 days.

The manor of Aller was held by Ednod in 1066 and, like Sampford, was held of Hugh d'Avranches, Earl of Chester, in 1086. The estate was held by Robert Brice and his wife by 1372 and was known as Aller Butler. It was passed down to John Sydenham, who sold Aller in 1568 to John Trevelyan, of Nettlecombe, in whose family it descended until 1804 when it was conveyed as part of a property exchange to the Earl of Egremont. Aller was occupied by four unmarried Wyndham brothers in the early-seventeenth century and at the time of writing by descendants of the Wyndham family, the farmland being let. The present house incorporated a cruck blade probably of the sixteenth century, but the building now appears to be mainly of the seventeenth century. The farm buildings are mainly of the nineteenth and twentieth centuries, former ones being damaged by fire. In 1851 Andrew Hosegood farmed 300 acres at Aller and employed 17 men, women and boys outdoors, as well as two servants and one nursemaid.

Tented camp of the West Somerset Yeomanry at Torweston, 1906.

SAMPFORD BRETT

Aller Farmhouse, near the western parish boundary, 1986. The pump for a private water-supply still exists within the house.

Behind the service station is the former Mill Farm, which had a water-powered flour mill.

Providence, a mill from 1820–64 and later a water pumping station until Clatworthy reservoir was opened to supply the village.

In 1833 the parish was said to produce good corn, vegetables and cider, and when Sir Peregrine Acland bought Torweston and most of the parish in 1846 the main crops were wheat, barley and vetches. In 1906 the chief crops were wheat, barley, mangolds, potatoes and turnips.

There were mills at Sampford and Torweston in 1086. Sampford Mill was held by John Strange in the 1660s and was often known as Strange's Mill during the eighteenth century. It continued in production in 1923, but had become Sampford Mill Farm by 1931. Remains of the old water-wheel and some of the workings are still there. Torweston Mill was mentioned in 1674, but was burnt down in about 1704. It was rebuilt as a grist mill with a fuller's stock adjoining and was part of Torweston Farm, being sited under where the railway track now runs. The mill house still standing at Torweston Farm was built in 1840 from local red sandstone and was still in use until 1958 when the tenant was Mr K.H. Pittard. The water which drove the mill wheel came from two lakes in front of the farmhouse, which are supplied from a spring in Luckes Lane. A 12-inch pipe ran from the larger lake under the road to the mill. An unusual feature of the mill is that the 18-foot-diameter wheel is situated below ground level. It is an overshot wheel which was turned by the weight of the water filling buckets. There was an indoor threshing machine, grinding stones, a reed-making machine, and a lighter shafting was used to power sheep shearing. The water-wheel and some machinery are still in the mill house.

Providence Mill was built in 1820, standing on the south-eastern edge of the village on the Doniford stream. Milling seems to have ceased there after 1864, but the building still stands and is used for residential purposes. In 1818 there was a leather mill at Catwell. Stone for the new tower of St Mary's Church, Taunton, and other prominent local buildings was procured from quarries near Sampford Brett.

St George's Church stands in a prominent position at the eastern end of the village and is built of stone, although parts are covered in pebble-dash. The church was mentioned in 1239 and the benefice was a sole rectory until 1978, when it became part of a united benefice with Bicknoller and Crowcombe; it is now part of the Quantock Towers Benefice.

The church was probably dedicated to St George by 1306 when Adam Brett was granted a fair at the feast of St George, and the building comprises a chancel with south vestry, nave with north transeptal chapel, south organ chamber, tower and west porch. The church was described as being of 'a very early character, Anglo-Norman', with lancet windows in the south wall of the chancel at its restoration. Its tower was constructed in the fourteenth century and the two great windows date from the same period. The bench-ends incorporate early-sixteenth century carved panels, probably set in their present position during the nineteenth century. A bench-end near the entrance commemorates Florence Wyndham, of Kentsford, who had the misfortune to be buried at St Decuman's, Watchet, whilst still alive. The sexton, looking for jewels, opened the coffin and was greeted by the corpse coming out of a coma! At this he fled, never to be seen again. Florence recovered and later went on to bear children. A seventeenth-century communion table is used as a side table, and the plate includes a cup and cover dated 1573.

From 1835–45 a major reconstruction of the church's interior took place, paid for by the Earl of Egremont.

View from the north-east of St George's Church, Sampford Brett.

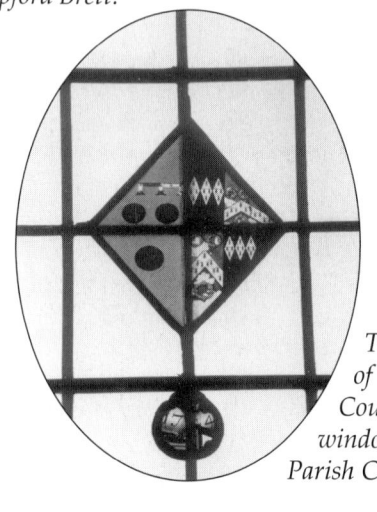
The stained glass coat of arms of Margaret de Courtenay in the west window of Sampford Brett Parish Church.

A bench-end in Sampford Brett Parish Church depicting Florence Wyndham and the twins she bore after her 'death'.

Brenda Knight at the console of the organ in Sampford Brett Parish Church, where she has been organist for 16 years, 2004.

SAMPFORD BRETT

Interior of St George's Church, Sampford Brett, c.1912. The organ is now situated in the south transept. Note the oil-lamps.

Sampford Brett bell-ringers, c.1920s. Left to right, back row: Arthur Groves, Albert Bulpin, Mr Furneaux, Arthur ('Forbes') Cavill, Albert Barker; front: Jack Bulpin, Arthur ('Arp') Jenkins, Charlie Jenkins.

Sampford Brett bell-ringers, 1962. Left to right: Richard Bulpin, Jack Vellacott, Jack Bulpin, Mervyn Arscott, Robert Yandle, Charlie Jenkins.

Sampford Brett bell-ringers, 1987. Left to right: Ken Whitfield, Joan Hopwood, ?, Robert Yandle, Winifred Kingsbury, Martin Blazey, Christine Pennington-Ridge.

SAMPFORD BRETT

The Rectory and garden, Sampford Brett, from the air, c.1990.

Central-heating radiators were installed in 1913 and electric lighting replaced oil-lamps and candles in 1935. Mr H.E. Davis of Monksilver fixed new leaded glass into the five war-damaged lights of the west window in 1957, the cost being paid for by the War Damage Commission. The registers are largely complete and date from 1629. In 1922 the duties of sexton were listed as: dig graves, cut the grass and keep the churchyard tidy, attend funerals and weddings, ring bell for services, light the lamps (32), open and close the church each day, light and stoke the fire, wind the clock. For this he was paid £10 a year; earlier that century it was £3. There was a chapel of ease at Aller at the end of the twelfth century.

Sampford Brett is fortunate in having one of the finest peals of six bells in West Somerset. The bells are positioned in the top third of the tower, access being gained by ladders and trapdoors, and are rung from the ground floor. The earliest record of a tenor bell is 1621. The clock, now electrically operated, is housed on the middle floor of the tower.

Known since 1978 as The Old Rectory, the former Rectory house was, until partial demolition of the south and west wings in 1903, built around a courtyard. The original medieval building was on the east side, with its kitchen at the south end. The house, which has large grounds, was extensively refitted in the early-nineteenth century and an inventory around 1839 indicates a substantial house with marble chimney-pieces in the principal rooms and a servants' hall. It was sold in 1978 and is now a private residence.

A Wesleyan Methodist 'Sunday place' had been established before 1827, but was given up in that year. Services were started again on Sundays in 1841, but were given up in 1844 because the farmers supported the chapel in Williton.

In 1818 there was a reading school with 15 pupils, and in 1835 15 children attended a day school, which was supported by parents. In 1867 St George's National School was built by Sir Alexander Acland-Hood for 100 children and also included a school house for the head teacher. On the school's opening a year later, 53 children were admitted, the parish's population being around 280 at that time. Sir Alexander let the school to the parish for £50 per year, which sum he gave back, and made himself responsible for school repairs, the laying on of water and dental treatment for the children. There were two teaching staff, and in 1904 the head teacher's salary was £65 per year and free board in the school house; the assistant teacher received £25 per year. In 1903 there were 64 children on the books and the school was also used for evening classes, Sunday school and confirmation classes.

Lord St Audries, the owner, gave notice to quit in 1924, but money was raised to buy the buildings. There were only eight children attending in 1933, and the school was closed in 1934. It was reopened for a short period at the outbreak of the Second World War owing to the arrival of a flood of evacuees. It is now a private residence, but still bears Sir Alexander's coat of arms.

From the 1930s to the '60s there was a private preparatory school named St Decuman's at Tower Hill. Its first head was Mr C.V. House, followed by Mr G. Small. At the time of writing it is known as Northfield House, a residential home for adults with hearing difficulties.

The village was almost self-contained in the nineteenth century with Aller Farm, Torweston Farm, Manor Farm, Francis Farm, Sampford Mill and Sully's at the bottom of Rocks; these employed 70 labourers. Also present in the village were dressmakers, cordwainers (shoemakers), carpenters, washer-women, as well as a mason, baker, butcher, tailor, thatcher, basket-maker and school mistress. George Langdon kept the village shop and Post Office and James Kerslake was blacksmith in the building now used as a motor repair shop near the present-day petrol service station by the main road. The position of the flue can still be seen on the rear wall of the old forge.

There was a licensed victualler in the parish in 1736. Tradition has it that Woodburnes (in former times known as Sully's Cottage), a centuries-old house on the left side of the village street from the direction of the church, may have been an alehouse. Behind the house is a detached two-storey, possibly seventeenth-century building, which may have been a brewhouse or bakehouse. Woodburnes originally had a thatched roof, but was replaced by tiling after it was destroyed by fire in 1928. Some of the wooden rafters remained after the fire and were of chestnut; no cob was found to have been used in the construction of the walls. In spite of extensive fire damage, part of the cruck structure and ancient roof remain. On the right side of the village street from the church is Francis Farm, which has been there since the seventeenth century, but much altered in the passage of time.

After the First World War it was thought that men discharged from the Forces should have a proper place to meet. An old Army hut was purchased for £260, the parish providing £113 and the remainder paid for by fund-raising activities. Some land adjacent to the school playground was given by Lord St Audries. Men of the village dug the foundations and erected the Hut; it was opened by Mr J. Tracey in 1921. The club was for men only with billiards, darts and cards being among the usual nightly activities; Mrs Welsher was the cleaner.

Northfield House, Tower Hill, 2002. It was formerly St Decuman's Preparatory School.

St Decuman's Preparatory School play, c.1940. Left to right, back row: Michael Street, Tony Yandle, Derek Gibbons, Ralph White, F. Maddock, Stephen Love, Chris Rew, Peter Hurford (later to become a brilliant organist); *front:* ? MacLachlan, ? Murray, J. Hickman, Peter Gregory, John England, ? Heseltine, ? Bird, H. Pittard, John Greswell.

SAMPFORD BRETT

The fire at Sully's Cottage (now known as Woodburnes) in July 1928 rendered two Sampford Brett families homeless. The ancient cottage had for long past been occupied by two families, there being separate staircases. The occupants were Mr T. Sully (owner) and his wife, with his tenant, Mr Alfred Gooding, his wife and three children. The alarm was raised just before 9a.m. by Ivy Welsher, who was fetching milk from Francis Farm for Mrs A.H. Jenkins. A call was put through to Minehead Fire Brigade and they arrived at 9.30a.m. The water in the little stream which runs through the village was inadequate to cope with the fire, so the engine was moved to the mill stream, a short distance from the church. This supply proved adequate, but the fire had become too deep-seated. In some places it was found that the thatch was over 2 feet thick. On the alarm being given at Williton, Mr T. Clarke (captain of Williton Fire Brigade) was driven to Sampford Brett. The standpipe and a quantity of hose belonging to the Williton brigade was procured, but it was discovered that the fire hydrant was of a different pattern to those at Williton and the standpipe could not be fixed to it! A standpipe brought by the Minehead brigade was tried and this could be fixed, enabling the Williton hose to be attached, thus providing an extra supply of water. The cause of the fire was never discovered.

Woodburnes, Sampford Brett, 2004.

In 1938 the Hut was also offered to the women of the village for one night a week and the Women's Social Club was founded. The Hut was little used during the early days of the Second World War with most of the menfolk being away on active service, and in 1942 the Ministry of Food rented the building until early 1945. It was in very poor condition when it was returned to the villagers and over the next few years fund-raising was done and voluntary help given to paint and repair the structure. During the late 1940s the Hut became known as the Village Hall. Adjacent land was given and in 1949 a kitchen and cloakrooms were built, and land for a car park was donated by Mr Yandle.

As the building aged, the committee decided that a new hall was the only answer. The first estimate to replace the Hut was £2,500 and fund-raising began in earnest and various grants sought. The final bill for the Village Hall was £13,000 – £4,900 was raised by the villagers and the remainder obtained from grants. A considerable amount of work, including demolition of the Hut, was carried out voluntarily. The stage was bought by Sampford Brett Players, now sadly disbanded.

The new Village Hall was opened by Mr Pollard, of the Rural Community Council for Somerset, in 1976, and during 1980–88 additional amenities were added. It is well supported and used for a wide variety of purposes – social and educational. It distinguished itself by winning the cup for the Best Kept Village Hall in West Somerset in 1978, 1979, 1986, 1987 and 1988; in 1988 it was also awarded the Championship Trophy for the whole of Somerset.

The Sampford Brett Art and Craft Exhibition was at one time one of the most eagerly awaited events in the yearly local social calendar. It was held in the Village Hall, but unfortunately was discontinued in 1997. Its chief instigators were the Revd and Mrs C.R.B. Coleman in 1962, but over the years was supported admirably by villagers and visitors alike.

Manor courts were held at Torweston in 1766. In 1836 the parish became part of Williton Poor Law Union, was in Williton Rural District from 1894 and became part of West Somerset District in 1974. Sampford Brett has had a Parish Council since 1961.

The Village Hall, Sampford Brett, 2004.

Village Personalities

Left: *Lifelong Sampford Brett resident Verena (Vera) Yandle in her robes as Dame of Grace of the Order of St John of Jerusalem. She was awarded this honour in 1989 for services to St John Ambulance. Miss Yandle has also been a lay reader, bell-ringer and for many years taught at the former St Audries Girls' School.*

Vera Yandle in her first long dress, c.1932.

Three teachers and a former headmistress of St Audries Girls' School, c.1970s. Left to right: Vera Yandle, Brenda Knight (head of music for 34 years), Cynthia Havergal (headmistress), Marion Winn.

Joan Jenkins (left) and Vera Yandle, c.1930s.

Mrs Bessie Bulpin (Sampford Brett's unofficial midwife) with Vera Yandle in the late 1920s.

Granny Bulpin (also known as 'Aunt Sarah'), of Sampford Brett.

Albert Bulpin with his son David sitting on Molly the horse, 1932.

Albert Bulpin, who ran a dairy and milk delivery business at Sampford Brett in the late 1920s, taking over from the Groves family. He later established the Beaconwood Dairy at Williton in the late 1940s.

Bessie Bulpin (left) and Emily Davis, c.1950s.

John Yandle, of Sampford Brett, 1955.

Sampford Brett-born Haydn Sully, who played cricket for both Somerset and Northamptonshire in the 1960s.

Left to right: Cyril, Alf and Fred Bulpin on their motorcycles at Sampford Brett, 1930.

Sampford Brett resident Eric Hill, who opened the batting with Harold Gimblett for Somerset in the late 1940s.

Local couple Jim and Floria (Florence) Welsher with their daughter Ivy, c.1917.

The Groves family, of Rose Cottage, c.1918. Left to right, back row: William Henry, Phyllis, Leonard, Hannah; front: Wilfred and Arthur.

The Groves children, of Rose Cottage, late 1920s. Left to right, back row: Leonard, Phyllis, Wilfred, Arthur; front: Victor and Bill.

Left to right: Stephen and Nigel (Wilfred Groves's sons), John and Colin (Leonard Groves's sons) in Sampford Brett School playground, 1944. The name of the goat is unknown!

The Jenkins family at Sampford Brett in the mid-1930s.

The Jenkins family in the 1940s. Left to right: Joe, Kathleen, Arthur, Sophie, Charlie, Nellie, John.

SAMPFORD BRETT

Right: *John Date, born in Sampford Brett in 1859, lived all his life in the village until his death in 1939.*

Far right: *Marjorie, Phyllis and Hilda Pearce outside Sampford Brett House, c.1940.*

Below: *Harry Isaac with Kimberley Richards at Torweston Farm, 1997.*

Above: *Fred Sully ploughing at Torweston in the 1940s.*

Charlie Jenkins, of Sampford Brett, with his team of grey shire horses at Woolston in the 1950s.

Amateur Dramatics

The village present Babes in the Wood *in the late 1940s. Left to right: Mrs Pittard, Mrs Richards, Miss Margaret Voss, Mrs Date.*

Babes in the Wood. *Left to right: Mrs Richards, Vera Yandle, Mrs Welsher, Cyril Date, Mrs Pittard.*

The Sampford Brett Players present The Man Outside, *1983. Left to right: Martin Blazey, Joyce Halliday, Mary Miller, David Wilson, Jane Whitfield, Norman Farmer.*

Babes in the Wood. *Left to right: Hugh Pittard, Vera Yandle, Leslie Sweetland.*

Below: *The village pantomime* Aladdin *in the late 1940s. Left to right: Mrs Dascombe, Mrs Welsher, Mrs Pittard, Mrs Richards, Miss Dascombe.*

SAMPFORD BRETT

Social Occasions

Sampford Brett Church Sunday school outing, c.1938. Among those pictured are: The Revd J.P.D. Forde, Violet Howe, Edith Pearce, Sophia Jenkins, Mrs Pearce, Barbara Ford, David Bulpin, Mary Bulpin.

Sampford Brett bell-ringers' outing to Berrow, 1948. Left to right: Arthur Jenkins, Bert Thorne, Charlie Jenkins, Nellie Jenkins, Harry Davis, Denis Davis (coach driver), Vera Yandle, Albert Bulpin, Arthur Cavill, Molly Vellacott (organist), Jack Bulpin, Gilbert Davis, Lewis Eslick. The boy in front is John Jenkins (son of Charlie).

Sampford Brett Mothers' Union, c.1950. Among those pictured are: Mrs Pittard, Phyllis Bulpin, Hilda Pearce, Mrs Bush, Emily Davis, Bessie Bulpin, Mrs Groves, Mrs Gillett, Mary Gillett.

Presentation at the harvest supper, 1968 to (left to right) Marjorie Bulpin, Charlie Jenkins, Hilda Pearce and Jack Bulpin on each completing over 50 years' service to the church.

Prizes at a fête on the Rectory lawn in the 1930s. Left to right: Revd J.P.D. Forde, Fred Grandfield (with sheep given by Mr J. Yandle), Alfred Bulpin, George Pearce (with wheelbarrow given by Mr A.H. Groves).

A group at the Sampford Brett Victorian Evening in the Village Hall, 1997. Left to right: Marion Winn, Jean Marsland, Nya Butler, Peggy Stradling.

A sing-along at a 1940s evening in Sampford Brett Village Hall, 1995.

SAMPFORD BRETT

The Sampford Brett Singers, 1998. Left to right, back row: Liz Blazey, Florence Plant, Mary Jeffery, Dylys Crabtree, Sheelagh Biddell, Peggy Stradling, Patricia Dening, Marion Winn, Kay Holder, Margaret Reed; front: Beryl Willes, Jane Whitfield, Shirley Waite, Hannah Gostling, Nya Butler, Jean Marsland, Gladys Fillary, Margaret Howard; seated at the piano: Kathleen Langley.

Sampford Brett Croquet Club, 1991. Left to right, back row: Charles Plant, Leslie Butler, John Gostling, Dorothy Royston, Glen Jeffery, Dot Clatworthy, Paul Biddell, Peggy March, Don Seckington, ?, Betty Wheeler, ?, ?, ?, Bob Reed, Ken Whitfield, Mary Campbell; front: Florence Plant, 'Bubbles' Poole, Jane Whitfield, Shirley Bates, Nya Butler, Margaret Reed, Celia West.

The Revd Charles Coleman (left), former rector, with Mrs Evelyn Coleman (exhibition founders) and Ken Whitfield (chairman of the Exhibition Committee) at the special celebration to mark the 25th anniversary of Sampford Brett's annual Arts and Crafts Exhibition in 1987. The exhibition was opened by Mr Coleman.

Garden fête at Sampford Brett, 1921.

Parish and People

Looking towards the church at Sampford Brett, c.1912.

Flood water outside No. 13, Sampford Brett, 1981. Left to right: Andy Norris, Robert Yandle, Charlie Jenkins, Dennis Knight, Richard Knight.

The main street in Sampford Brett under water, 1981.

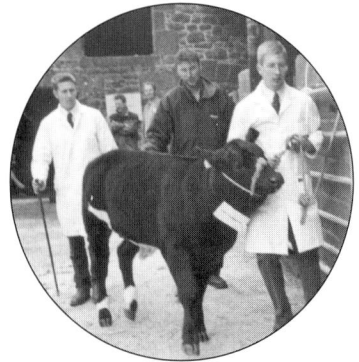

Keith Richards leading his prize bullock, 'Bandit', at a Young Farmers' rally at Torweston Farm in 2003.

Nos 10 and 11, Sampford Brett, c.1930s.

SAMPFORD BRETT

Sampford Brett looking eastwards, c.1950.

Above left: *One of the three concealed doors connecting No. 13, Sampford Brett, to Ivy Cottage next door, discovered during renovations in 1991. This lends credence to the belief that the cottages were originally one longhouse and not built as individual residences. Parts of the building date from the fifteenth century and parts from Victorian times. During the renovations also discovered was a well outside the back door of Ivy Cottage, which is thought to date from Elizabethan times because of the very small bricks around its head.*
Above right: *After the fireplace was removed at No. 13, showing the discovery of two bread ovens and a beam dating from between 1480–1520.*

Francis Farmhouse, Sampford Brett, c.1950. The village shop and Post Office is on the left.

The garden path at Rose Cottage (now known as Brett Water Cottage) looking towards the school, early 1930s.

Manor (previously Sampford) Farm, 1987.

Mr J. Yandle's sale at Manor Farm, 1953.

Snowbound Sampford Brett, 1962.

Children inspecting icicles at Sampford Brett in 1962.

Children fishing the stream in Maggie's Field, 1959.

Leslie Sweetland giving Richard Bulpin and Reg Hankey a ride on Mr Yandle's horse Prince, 1949.

Alfred Bulpin with his brother's (Mr A.E. Bulpin) milk float after winning first prize at Williton Gymkhana in 1929.

A small plane forced to make a landing in a field at the top of Rocks, 1949. Left to right: Donald Pearce, George Pearce, Alfred Bulpin, Richard Bulpin, Ann Chaplin, Kathleen and Reg Hankey.

Rose Cottage (now Brett Water Cottage), 1930.

Workmen of J. Chibbett & Sons, Williton, with ladies at the building of Overbridge bungalow, 1953. Left to right: Percy Webber, Laurence Chorley, Alfred Bulpin, David Salter, Phyllis Bulpin, Mrs Francis, Jack Chidgey, Miss Greening.

Bulpin's Cottage (on right), Sampford Brett, c.1950.

Landlocked Sampford Brett was the starting point for the debut journey of a massive Dutch barge in March 2004. It was built by Mark Vardy, of the Quantock Service Station, who has been building and fitting out narrow boats for some time. Mark, whose boating sideline trades under the name Little Mouse Inc., moved up a scale with the barge venture. The 70 feet by 14 feet barge, worth around £250,000 and weighing approximately 60 tons, was craned out of the service station site onto the back of a trailer to make its way to Portishead where it was to be launched. The three-bedroom, sea-going boat, complete with kitchen, bathroom and wheelhouse-dining area, will be used in a new charter business. Initially, it will travel the River Avon to Stratford, but eventually it is hoped it will be taken across the Channel to work the Continental inland waterways. The barge is pictured being lifted by a large crane from its building site at the rear of the Quantock Service Station onto a lorry trailer for the start of its journey.

SAMPFORD BRETT

Brook House (originally Brook Farm), which is approximately 200 years old.

Left: *A small remaining segment of the mill-race which used to supply the flour mill at Mill Farm, 1987.*

Right: *Part of the tributary of the Doniford stream which runs through the centre of the village.*

The tithe barn, of uncertain age.

The old limekiln, south of Sampford House, on Stogumber Hill.

The old village pump.

Robin and Margaret Reed outside what is thought to have been the brewhouse for the adjoining reputed alehouse (now known as Woodburnes), 2004.

The aftermath of a devastating explosion at fifteenth-century Rose Cottage, Capton, in 1998. The cottage was totally destroyed by the blast as Williton and Wiveliscombe fire crews were tackling a blaze inside the property. Six firemen, including sub-officer Nigel Ridler and Martin Nicholas, both of Williton, and neighbour June Rexworthy were hospitalised by the incident. Some of the firemen sustained very serious injuries and burns, but thankfully all eventually recovered after a lengthy period. A total of six fire appliances attended, as well as special back-up from Taunton and Bridgwater. It was thought that lightning in the early hours started a fire inside the cottage, which was empty at the time as owners Robert and Ann Wright were holidaying in France. The lightning bolt caused an electrical surge to enter the cottage which led to the rupture of a propane gas supply pipe. Ignition of the gas occurred as the two village crews were entering the cottage to make a search.

The rebuilt Rose Cottage at Capton with salvaged stone from the old building used for the external finish. The thatch roof was replaced by one of natural slate.

Did this Chest Belong to Elizabeth Courtenay?

The discovery in 2000 of an elm-boarded, six-plank, eighteenth-century chest in an old cider barn by owner Miss Brenda Knight, of Sampford Brett, has created something of a mystery as to its original owner. The contents of the barn, which still contains the cider press, had probably not been disturbed for at least 40 years. Obviously locally made, the coffer's flower decoration is a fairly typical West Country design, and has cross-hatching or nail-head decoration in the centre of each flower. The same cross-hatching decoration is to be found on an early-sixteenth century bench-end in the Parish Church of St Mary the Virgin at East Quantoxhead.

The three flowers which decorate the front of the coffer have a letter 'E' to their left and a letter 'C' on their right. In 1359 Hugh Courtenay, Earl of Devon, and his wife Margaret bought the Sampford Brett and Torweston estates, which remained with the family for nearly 500 years. In 1743 the estates passed to a descendant of the family, Elizabeth Courtenay, who married John Chichester, of Arlington. She had spent her early years in Devon, but it is not known how much of their lives Elizabeth and John spent at Sampford Brett.

As the dates for the making of the coffer and the time Elizabeth inherited the Sampford Brett and Torweston estates coincide, it is a strong possibility that at one time the chest was owned by Elizabeth Courtenay. The carving of the 'E' for Elizabeth and the 'C' for either Courtenay or Chichester certainly lends credence to this theory.

The old cider barn in which the chest was discovered.

The chest as it was when discovered...

... and after restoration.

Apple breaker (above) *and cider press* (below) *in an old barn at Sampford Brett.*

Vision at the Rectory

During a visit to Sampford Brett Rectory by the local Archive Group in May 2004 when the Rectory was up for sale, archive member Martin Southwood had the following conversation with Rectory owner David Luckett:

David: *Going back a long while ago in the Rectory, I was with my mother and we were walking from the kitchen, when out of the right-hand corner room, which was a cold room (a storage room for meat) I saw a vision of a lady who was dressed in a maid's outfit and was quite old and disappeared through a wall. I subsequently found out from the history of the building that there was a maid at the Rectory who used to live in the cottage next door – which was the maid's quarters.*

Martin: *What sort of year would that have been?*

David: *It's going back to Victorian times.*

Martin: *No, I mean when did you see her?*

David: *This was in, I think, 1982. I clearly saw her; it was just like looking at someone coming out.*

Martin: *And she would have been in old garb?*

David: *Yes, very old clothing, which startled me. I had to look twice, but saw her very clearly.*

Martin: *Long skirt?*

David: *Yes, went right down to the ground, and she was quite old. She wasn't young.*

Martin: *Housekeeper?*

David: *Possibly. I later found out that there was a way [access] from the maid's quarters – there was a private door upstairs. Five years later we found the private door from the cottage next door to the main Rectory, and that was all boarded and bricked up.*

During recent renovations at The Old Rectory we trust the old maid's spirit was not unduly disturbed!

A ghostly vision; a sketch by Michael Chapman.

Arthur Jenkins sitting proudly on his Raleigh motorcycle, 1932.

The Tailor of Sampford Brett

Few men can have been more part and parcel of Sampford Brett life than Arthur Henry Jenkins (who was affectionately known as 'Arp'), the village tailor. He was a real 'church and parish man', one who had his native Sampford Brett 'under his ken' all his life. He loved the village and wider spheres of more lucrative pastures had never appealed to him. Mr Jenkins had never been to London, and a visit he made to Minehead in 1950 when he and Mrs Jenkins (formerly Sophia Anne Thorne, daughter of a shepherd at Torweston) celebrated their golden wedding, was his first for about 15 years.

Ever since he left school at the age of 13 he had been tailoring in the room at No. 13 where his father had sat cross-legged before him. Mr Jenkins was helped in his trade by his wife, who had learned dressmaking in Williton. He left his work only for relaxation at a football match, usually at Williton, or to attend to one of his manifold duties at St George's Church, where he could almost be said to be part of the very fabric.

Arthur Jenkins was the youngest and last surviving of the five sons of Charles Jenkins, Sampford Brett's tailor of more than a century ago. Indeed, it was as a young man of 21, around the end of the nineteenth century, that Arthur succeeded to the business on his father's death, and he carried it on in good and bad times. He could recall, as a breeches maker, finding the material, cutting and making, then delivering the goods several miles, for the princely sum of 12s.6d. (63p). He and his wife had never had a full week's holiday in their lives. Arthur once spent a month in Bristol learning cutting and had quite enough of the bright lights of the city, returning to his birthplace to leave it no more.

The following extracts from Mr Jenkins's accounts ledger make fascinating reading:

Arthur Jenkins cutting Louis Bulpin's hair, c.1940. Louis was tragically killed in a road accident at St Audries in 1949.

15 July 1899:   Revd O. Sadler, pair spats, 7s.6d.; footman's livery, £3.18s.

19 May 1906:	Mr A.E. Hyett, Stogumber, trousers, 14s.; Mr J. Bulpin, Sampford Brett, best tweed suit, £2.5s.; Mr F. Symes, Capton, making and trimming suit, 17s.; Mr A. Cavill, Capton, blue serge suit, £1.12s.; Mr P. Hutchings, Williton, knickers, 16s.; Mr Charles Durie, Sampford Brett, white flannel trousers, 12s.6d., and repairing cricket bag, 3d.
1 January 1921:	Mr A. Cavill, Williton, tweed coat, £3.3s.; Mr H.F. Groves, Sampford Brett, cord breeches, £2.3s.
25 March:	Mr Wm Jones, Williton, blue suit, £5.5s.
8 April	Mr J. Date, Sampford Brett, tweed suit, £5.10s.

Mr Jenkins's remarkable connection with his Parish Church dates from the time when his father, who always wore a top hat, introduced him to the then fashionable ways of strict Sabbatarianism, and hauled him along at the age of six to St George's about three or four times each Sunday. From being a choirboy he went on to adult service in the stalls for a record of more than 65 years. He was a verger for about 33 years and a bell-ringer for 65, being captain of the tower band, and taught the ringing art to many others. He wound the church clock for more than 30 years, and was a sidesman in addition to all his other duties, which were always performed with the punctilious sense of responsibility that was part of his nature. He enjoyed such remarkably good health that his absence was unthinkable.

In view of such outstanding service it was fitting that a special service should be held for Mr and Mrs Jenkins at St George's Church, where they had married, on the occasion of their golden wedding. Mr Jenkins knew St George's when there were 32 lamps and candles to light and when the village school, now closed, was packed with over 100 pupils. He was also the village barber, and took an active part in all social life.

Arthur Jenkins died in 1953 at the age of 76. He was the father of Frederick Charles (Charlie) Jenkins, who died in 1990, aged 87. Charlie, a jovial, larger than life character, had also resided in Sampford Brett all his life at No. 13 and died in the same cottage. On leaving school at the age of 14 he went to work for Mr Langdon at Francis Farm, where he remained until his retirement in 1967. Following in his father's footsteps, he was a keen churchgoer and in 1981 emanated his father by completing 65 years as a bell-ringer. Charlie was taught to ring when he was 14 and in 1953 was appointed tower captain, sexton and verger in succession to his father. His other great love was horses and the beloved grey shires with which he worked for many years were his pride and joy. A quarter peal of Bob Doubles was rung as a thanksgiving for his life.

Early Memories of a Local Bell-Ringer

The authors are grateful to Gilbert Davis for the following article. Gilbert spent his early life at Sampford Brett, where he had a long apprenticeship in the science of bell-ringing. After completing his National Service in the Army, Gilbert returned home for a while but then joined the Somerset and Avon Constabulary and now lives in retirement with his wife Molly at Bridgwater. As well as bell-ringing, Gilbert now keeps himself busy painting watercolours.

I was born in 1932 at No. 10, Sampford Brett. In those days life was very much different. There were only three cars in the village – one owned by the rector, the Revd J.P.D. Forde; one by Mr Garle, who lived at Elmfield; and a third by Mr Albert Bulpin, the local milkman.

The cottages were occupied by farm workers, as far as I remember. Ten were employed at Torweston, four by Mr Yandle of Manor Farm and Charlie Jenkins by Mr Langdon at Francis Farm; there was also the Grandfield family, who worked Sampford Mill and farmed its acres. The mill's water-wheel was driven by a leat which was diverted from the main stream near Providence Cottages, then flowed through the fields and the orchard near the church, under the road near the service station, and on beside the road to the mill. Tractors were rare indeed before the war and nearly all the work was undertaken by horses, of which the best turned out were the ones in the charge of Charlie Jenkins.

One of my earliest memories is of the rector driving his Austin car up the lane alongside Manor Farm towards Capton to take the rogation service in the field known as Home Piece. This custom stopped on the outbreak of war in 1939, as did the custom of ringing the Death Knell or the Nine Tailors as it is sometimes known.

Mrs Langdon ran the village Post Office and shop, adjoining the Rectory drive. There was then a wide paved path to the shop which, together with the dividing wall, has disappeared and the old shop door is no longer. Mrs Langdon sold sweets from large jars as well as cheese and groceries. My abiding memory was of the large and loud bell which went 'clang' as one opened the door.

I commenced school at Williton in 1937 but, owing to the arrival of many evacuees, the village school at Sampford Brett

Charlie Jenkins, 1987.

was reopened and for a time I attended there with the other village children, being taught by some of the London teachers. The school was closed again as most of the evacuees returned home as the war passed through the 'phoney' stage.

These are hazy recollections and I could be wrong on points. Not so the night when two land mines dropped near the village – one in a field at Brimball, to the right of the footpath to Williton; the other in a field known as Woodshill, to the west of Manor Farm. The blast from the latter explosion did great damage to the buildings at Manor Farm and throughout the village, removing the west end window of the village church. Luckily there were no casualties, although a deep crater was formed which, despite great efforts to fill it in, can still be seen to this day. Great quantities of parachute silk and shrapnel were found when the nearby fields were harvested.

My contemporaries and I were roped into the choir. However, unlike my father, I could not sing! I could – and still do – make an out of tune noise, so St George's Church Choir did not want me. So, in true British tradition, I was promoted – to organ blower. This I continued for some years, adding my name to the list of others on the pump side of the old organ. I had got into the habit of escaping via the south door, where I read a book, sat on the table tomb near this door. One sunny, warm Sunday towards the end of the war, the rector's sermon was short – maybe he wanted to escape! I suspect now he was not well. Suddenly he announced the final hymn and the lady at the organ started to play – no sound, no air, and no organ blower! A quick search party found me and the service concluded. Within a very short time an electric blower was fitted, shortly to be followed by the gift of a new organ. Myself, out on my ear, was shown the belfry door by Mr Arthur Jenkins. I remember I had no chance to say No, but was given the rope of the Old Third and told to pull.

The bells at this time were the five that had been recast in 1894 and hung by John Sully, of Stogumber, in a reconstructed frame at the very top of the tower, reached by two wooden ladders. The upper chamber, through the clock room, creaked and groaned and to me was terrifying. During the war the bells were silent, but the band at this time were the same as pre-war, with Mr Arthur Jenkins as tower captain. He had been the village tailor for his whole life and was the only member of the band to have rung in a peal of 5,040 changes. The tailor's shop, where Arthur could be seen sitting cross-legged on his bench in true tailor tradition, was also the village meeting place where news was exchanged.

Another ringer was his son Charles, who normally rang the fourth bell. He was the carter at Francis Farm where he looked after his beautiful grey horses, and in later years followed his father as captain. Jack Bulpin usually rang the third; he was a farm worker for Mr John Yandle at Manor Farm and lived next door to my family at No. 11. Albert Bulpin lived at Croft House, but later moved his dairy business to Beaconwood at Williton, which I think had been a private school. Arthur Cavill also lived at Williton and was the senior ringer after Arthur Jenkins and always rang the tenor, calling the touches which we rang. My father, Harry Davis, usually rang the treble.

I had a long apprenticeship, most of my first winter being spent on bells which had been silenced. I first had to learn to raise and lower a bell, follow another silent bell, dodge, and do every manoeuvre possible. As a result when I came to ring an open bell I could already ring passable rounds. Methods rung were mainly Grandsire and Plain Bob Doubles, but later we progressed to St Simon Doubles and rang a little Steadman Striking, which was always excellent.

There was always great rivalry between Sampford Brett and Stogumber bell-ringers, who could hear each other's bells. I remember our band was extremely critical. Visits were made to other towers – Stogumber, Crowcombe, St Audries and Monksilver in the main – mostly travelling by pedal cycle. On one memorable occasion in the late 1940s we went via Bryant's Coach to ring at Berrow.

As bell-ringing resumed after the war, I started to attend Association meetings and as such came to know other ringers. By the time I reached 18 years of age in 1950 I could ring several minor, triple and major methods on six and eight bells. I commenced my National Service at Aldershot in June 1950 and my ringing ability served me well there and at Farnham. I later rang with bands at Portsmouth and in Shropshire before returning to live at home in June 1952. But by this time the ringing had changed – I think it was the end of an era.

Gilbert Davis, c.1985.

Royal Occasions

Sampford Brett Coronation programme, 1937.

Richard Bulpin in 2004 beside a wheelbarrow made by Sampford Brett carpenter and craftsman Albert Groves to commemorate the Coronation of Queen Elizabeth II in 1953. It was originally painted in patriotic colours and decorated with Union Jacks.

Watching a Punch and Judy show at a fête to celebrate the Golden Jubilee of Queen Elizabeth II, 2002.

Coronation Celebrations, 1953

Two television sets installed in the Village Hut afforded Sampford Brett parishioners an eye-catching view of the Coronation of Queen Elizabeth II on Tuesday 2 June 1953. This was the foremost part of the village's arrangements for the celebrations. From 10.30a.m. until mid-afternoon the television sets, provided by Mr E.G. Ashman, of Williton, were in operation and gave great pleasure to a good number of people assembled in the decorated Hut.

Earlier in the morning parishioners attended a service at St George's Church conducted by the rector, the Revd V.G. Havergal Shaw. A sports programme was carried out in the afternoon under the supervision of Messrs J. Richards, C. Jenkins and J. Vellacott.

After the sports, a high tea was provided for all parishioners, arranged by Mrs A. Sully, Mrs K.H. Pittard and other lady helpers. The presentation of prizes for the sports and Coronation souvenirs to the children was made by Mrs V.G. Havergal Shaw. Also presented to the children were a pencil and commemoration book entitled 'Elizabeth, our Queen'.

In the evening Les Amery's Band was in attendance at a social and dance to play for old-time and modern dancing and games, Mr J. Richards being MC. A feature of the evening was the cutting of a large cake, followed by a toast to the Queen.

Members of the committee who made the arrangements for the day, other than those previously mentioned, were Messrs K.H. Pittard (chairman), E.W. Price (secretary), E. Hemmer (treasurer), Mrs J. Welsher, Mrs C. Date, Miss M. Vellacott, Mrs M. Hogben, the Revd V.G. Havergal Shaw, Mrs M. Palk, Mr H. Davis and Mr F.J. Hogben.

Extracts from Sampford Brett CE School Logbooks, 1868-1934

The following extracts make fascinating reading and reflect wider social changes. No names have been mentioned here where embarrassment might be caused. The school was closed in 1934, but was reopened for a while at the beginning of the Second World War to help cope with the influx of evacuees. The logbooks are kept at the Somerset Record Office at Taunton.

1868
- *20 April:* St George's National School, Sampford Brett, opened; 53 children admitted. Only seven boys and four girls were able to write their names.
- *22 April:* Six more children admitted, two of whom were girls, 9 and 10 years. None were able to write.
- *1 June:* Mary Jane Milton commenced being a monitor. Revd John Tripp visited the school.
- *8 July:* Being the Royal Foresters' Fete, only 33 children were present in the morning.

1869
- *15 Feb:* Sir Alexander Acland-Hood came to the school in the morning.
- *22 March:* Mary Date, Albert Shears and Alfred Morse did their writing very nicely.
- *6 April:* Chief teacher, Sibylla Tennant; monitor, Elizabeth Tennant.
- *27 April:* School report: 'This school, recently opened in new and commodious buildings under a certificated mistress, is likely to be of great benefit to the population around. The discipline is well maintained.'

1870
- *14 March:* Ernest Shears, aged two years and two months, admitted.
- *21 July:* Broke up for harvest vacations for five weeks.
- *2 Sept:* Average attendance very small, most of the elder children being away picking apples.

1871
- *28 July:* Annie Jane Stevens resigned as chief teacher.
- *23 Sept:* Annie Preece appointed chief teacher.
- *13 Oct:* Sixty-six present this week. A boy punished for taking one of the other children's dinner.

1872
- *31 May:* Gave a holiday on Monday as there were only 10 children present in the morning owing to the Club Festival at Williton.

1873
- *9 April:* Attendance small this week as several of the children are planting potatoes.
- *12 June:* Annie Preece resigned her situation as chief teacher.
- *23 June:* Ellen Mary Mann appointed chief teacher; pupil teacher, Fanny White.
- *12 July:* Several of the older children absent this week – at work in the fields.
- *8 Aug:* Some of the older children absent this week – picking whortleberries.

1874
- *6 Feb:* Mrs Gould gave 4s.6d. worth of buns to the children.

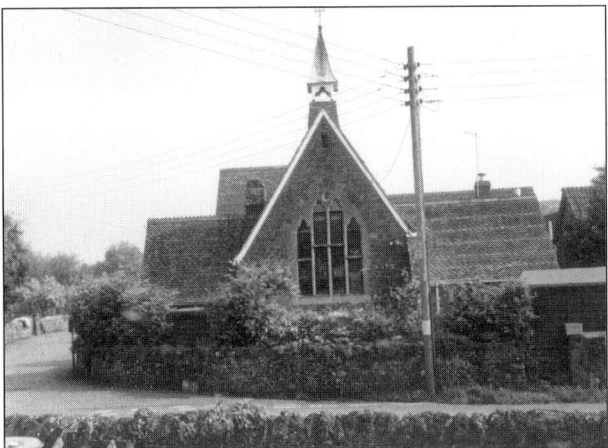

The old school (now a private residence), Sampford Brett, 2004.

1875
29 Oct: A very small attendance; many children required for picking apples and potatoes.

1876
15 Sept: A holiday was given for the children to attend the Harvest Home.

1877
23 Oct: A full school, 78 present in the morning.

1878
25 May: Average attendance 73.

1879
8 May: Inspector's report: 'This school is decidedly above the average of country schools.'
16 May: Not many present on account of the otter hunt.

1880
16 Sept: No school in the afternoon as there was a Harvest Home in the village.

1881
30 Jan: No school this morning owing to the snow drifts.

1882
11 Oct: The mistress sent two boys home to wash their hands and faces.

1883
10 April: A good many of the boys in Standard V absent planting potatoes.
4 May: Average attendance 79.
25 June: No school in the afternoon owing to a circus performance in Williton.

1884
15 Oct: Punished several children for coming to school with dirty hands.

1885
4 Nov: Gave an examination to all the children and found the spelling bad throughout.

1886
13 April: Several boys absent planting potatoes.
5 Oct: Average attendance 61.

1887
16 March: Only 29 present on account of heavy snow.
21 July: Several of the older children absent picking whortleberries.

1888
10 Jan: Retained several of the children after school for carelessness in arithmetic.

1889
8 March: No school in the afternoon on account of the streets being flooded.

The coat of arms of the Acland-Hood family on a wall of the old school at Sampford Brett.

1 Nov: All the boys' pockets were cleared of apples this afternoon. For the past week rules have been violated by bringing apples to the room and eating them during lessons.

1890
23 May: Inspector's report: 'This school has fallen away very much, both as regards discipline and attainments of the scholars...'
18 July: A cricket club has been started for the schoolboys through the kindness of the Revd J. Tripp and other friends.

1891
2 Oct: Admitted Alfred Cavill from Capton.
16 Oct: Average attendance 41.

1892
11 Nov: Average attendance 35.

1893
24 March: Florence Morse, Ellen Bulpin and Frank Stevens have been at home for some time through illness.
7 Dec: Owen Grandfield went home at 10 o'clock – very poorly.

1894
20 July: Several children absent from school – picking whortleberries on the hills.

1895
26 April: Inspector's report: 'An excellent year's work has been done, and the school is in first rate order as regards both discipline and attainment.'

1898
22 Feb: Snowing nearly all the day. The children did not come to school.

1899
12 April: Annie Gould, aged 12 years, who sat last month at Williton for the Ellsworth Charity, has obtained an exhibition of £5.
14 Sept: Sir Alexander Acland-Hood, Bart, on behalf of the managers and other subscribers, presented a testimonial, consisting of a marble clock, to Mr B. Angwin on his resignation of the mastership of this school after seven years of faithful and efficient service.

1900
8 Jan: Commenced school again – 58 present.
26 Feb: Annie Gould commenced duties as monitress.
1 March: On receiving the news of the relief of Ladysmith this morning, the children went outside the school and, on the hoisting of the Union Jack on the tower, sang 'God Save the Queen' and gave cheers for Lord Roberts, Generals Buller and

SAMPFORD BRETT

22 March: *White, and our soldiers in South Africa.*
In the recent Ellsworth examination Annie Gould came out first on the list of the whole number of candidates.

1901
22 Feb: *At the Ellsworth examination, Alfred Cavill and Herbert Perry are the candidates from this school.*
15 July: *Admitted Louis Bulpin, Gladys Date and Elsie Bosley – infants.*

1902
6 June: *Ethel Cavill, Arthur Thomas, Fred Ware, Gladys Sawyer, Fred Symes, Frank Gould, Arthur Cavill, Willie Sully and Lena Proll obtained first class passes and prizes in the recent Diocesan prize examination; Florrie Cavill and Blanche Perry were commended.*
9 June: *Attendance 52.*

1903
7 March: *A police constable from Williton questioned some of the boys about some damage to water pipes.*
2 Sept: *A girl had to be sent home to get her head, which was in a filthy state, cleaned.*
6 Oct: *There are no exercise or drawing books, slates or pencils in stock.*
21 Dec: *Blanche Perry, aged 12, died yesterday after a few days' illness. We are much grieved.*

1904
5 Sept: *Admitted William Hawkins and Irene Bosley.*

1905
4 Sept: *Admitted Alfred Bulpin, Annie Stevens, Churlie Jenkins and Winifred Thorne. Number on register 53.*

1906
8 June: *The week has been a trying one, owing to a spirit of rebellion among the boys of four families.*
20 Sept: *Admitted Leonard Bulpin.*

1907
26 March: *Nellie Bulpin received her certificate of exemption for five years' good attendance, being 13 today.*
20 Sept: *Number on books 41.*
12 Dec: *Today school could not assemble on account of the flood, making the roads impassable.*

1908
21 Feb: *Report of HM Inspector: 'The work of this school cannot be regarded as satisfactory. The children are unable to answer the simplest common sense questions in arithmetic; geography has been taught without reference to maps or atlases, and the older children, though they may be able to read, do not appear to be able to gather information for themselves...'*
26 March: *Alice Bulpin, Tower Hill, left school, 14 years old.*

1909
13 Jan: *Admitted Albert Bulpin.*

1910
27 July: *Children dismissed early to attend a flower show at Williton.*
16 Sept: *Admitted George Henry Perry.*

1911
17 March: *Thomas Bulpin has passed the examination for a Labour Certificate.*
7 April: *Admitted Geoffrey Date this week; Gladys Date has left school.*
19 May: *Admitted Frances Furneaux (infant) this week.*
3 July: *Several children away all day picking whortleberries.*

1912
9 Feb: *Received notice that the cookery class for the elder girls will commence at Williton on 19 February.*
16 Sept: *Reopened after harvest holiday – 32 present.*
20 Sept: *Admitted Stanley Date.*

1913
23 Jan: *Two children away all week with bad feet.*
27 June: *Admitted Bertha Chorley.*
10 July: *Admitted Winifred Ford.*

1914
25 Feb: *Mr T. Hosegood visited this morning.*
29 May: *Several children excluded owing to ringworm.*

1915
26 March: *Admitted Arthur Yandle.*
6 Sept: *Admitted Mabel Grandfield.*

1916
28 March: *Very snowy roads – only 20 present.*
18 Sept: *School reopened after summer holiday – 37 present.*

1917
6 July: *Very poor attendance in infant room owing to whooping cough and bad colds.*
30 Nov: *Prizes for essays on the Great War were awarded to Phyllis Groves and Bertha Chorley.*

1918
7 Jan: *Admitted Margaret Chorley.*
9 Sept: *Admitted Winifred Long and Edith Blackmore.*
1 Nov: *Admitted Marjorie and Phyllis Pearce.*
4 Nov: *Winners of prizes given by the Hon. Mrs Tracey for the best letters written to her: Spencer Lyddon in Group 1 and Fred Grandfield in Group 2. Alfred Bulpin received a consolation prize.*

1919
26 March: *Admitted Ellen Appleby.*
15 Sept: *Reopened school – 44 present.*

1920
23 Jan: *Winifred, Violet and Albert Nicholls have been*

3 Nov:	unable to attend during the past fortnight as the road from their home has been practically impassable. The Hon. Mrs Tracey and Miss Greswell visited this afternoon.

1921

12 July:	Twenty children went to the dentist at Williton.
23 Sept:	With the exception of Violet Howe, who is ill, the children have made perfect attendance this week.

1922

28 Feb:	Holiday given for Princess Mary's wedding.
27 March:	Readmitted John Furneaux.
19 May:	Half holiday given for children to attend circus at Williton.

1923

26 April:	A holiday given on account of the wedding of the Duke of York.
18 June:	Extract from report of the Diocesan Examiner: 'This school has recently become a junior school for children under 11 years of age...'
3 Sept:	Commenced school after summer holidays. Mabel Grandfield and Florence Chorley, both being 11 years of age, have gone to Williton school. Admitted Doris May Stone.
3 Oct:	Admitted Albert Baker.
1 Nov:	Constance M. Saville commenced duties as headmistress of this school.
26 Nov:	Admitted Gordon Voss, John Davey, Dorothy and Mildred Welsher.

1924

14 Jan:	Admitted Dorothy Alma Rose.
19 March:	Miss Jennings has been appointed as an uncertificated teacher.
1 April:	Number of children on roll 24. Audrey Binding and Edna Tompkins admitted.
29 April:	Clifford Symes readmitted.
2 Sept:	School reopened. Victor Groves, Cyril Grandfield, Vera Bryant and Ernest Hawkins admitted.

1925

6 Jan:	School reopened. Number on roll 28.
13 March:	Willie and Victor Groves have been excluded from school this week as they both show symptoms of mumps.
24 April:	Miss C.M. Jennings has left the staff of this school today.
30 April:	C.M. Saville resigned as headmistress.
1 May:	Ellen Lamming commenced duties as headmistress. Miss C. Churchill also started in the infants' room.
22 May:	The Revd H. Christian Young examined the school in Scripture this morning.
11 Nov:	Armistice Day was observed.

1926

26 Feb:	Lily Sweetland admitted. Number on books is now 30.
30 July:	During the last month the majority of the scholars have been very restless and difficult to manage and their progress has not been satisfactory. This is chiefly due to want of sufficient sleep, the children being frequently about the village long after nine o'clock. Complaints to their parents are of no avail.

1927

26 April:	Miss Ashman commenced her duties as supplementary teacher.

Schoolchildren and teacher watching the fire at Sully's Cottage (now known as Woodburnes), 1928.

SAMPFORD BRETT

1928
23 Oct: Visited the Museum at Taunton with seven older children for a history lesson.

1929
29 May: Barbara Lamming, aged 11 years, has been successful in obtaining a County Scholarship – the first occasion on which a pupil from this school has succeeded.
5-9 Dec: School was closed on these days on account of floods.

1930
25 May: Edna Tompkins, aged 11, has passed Part I of the County Scholarship examination.
11 Nov: Children listened to service broadcast from the Cenotaph.

1931
April: Report from HM Inspector: 'The headmistress of this little junior school continues to do excellent work. The arithmetic and English of the older children is now much above the average for their age and it is not surprising to find that in each of the last two years a free place has been secured at the local secondary school...'
21 July: Margaret Lamming has passed the County Scholarship and will proceed to Minehead County Secondary School.
31 Dec: I resigned my position as headmistress today – Ellen Lamming.

1932
11 Jan: I, Ethel V. Swanson, have taken temporary charge of this school today. Ten children present.
10 Feb: Received a letter from the office asking for reason of Vera Yandle's attendance here, as she is over 11 years of age. Letter referred to the Rector.
25 March: I resign charge today – E.V. Swanson.
4 April: Commenced duties as mistress of this school – Leonora M. Hearne.
29 April: Victor Groves has passed Part I of the County Scholarship examination.
22 June: Victor Groves has passed the County Scholarship examination and will proceed to Minehead County Secondary School.

1933
24 Feb: School closed today on account of snow.
31 Aug: Miss L. Hearne left today for another appointment.
18 Sept: I have today taken over charge of this school – D. Johnson. Number on register, 7.
16 Oct: Yard broom, enamel bowl and jug, etc, supplied by Parsons & Hann, Williton.
24 Nov: Little Margaret Voss absent all the week – her daddy died on Sunday and she had to be sent away to friends for a week. Last evening after dark little Freddie Eslick, the baby of the school, met with a serious road accident and was taken by ambulance to the Minehead Hospital.
8 Dec: Attendance very poor – Margaret Voss away three days; Leslie Sweetland away all the week.
20 Dec: Freddie Eslick is still in hospital but has made a remarkable recovery.

1934
9 Jan: Number on roll, 7. Both rooms very cold. Freddie Eslick is now at home and remarkably well.
15 Jan: Only two children present. Gerald Grandfield absent under doctor's orders, his brother has scarlet fever, Milly Eslick has measles, Margaret Voss suffering from a very severe cold (measles suspected), and Sidney Moles was ill during the weekend.
19 March: A letter from the County Education Secretary dated 16 March informed me that the committee are arranging to close the school at the end of this term.
21 March: The headmaster of Williton CE School, Mr W.J. White, came this afternoon to confer with me over the furniture, books, new stock, etc, which might be useful in his school.

The following are some of the pupils whose names appeared in the school registers over the years: Albert Bulpin, Ronald Chorley, Mabel Grandfield, Mabel Carrott, Phyllis Groves, Leonard Groves, Joyce Boyles, Wilfred Groves, Ivy Welsher, Margaret Chorley, John Furneaux, Donald Voss, William Groves, Samuel Gadd, Dorothy Welsher, Mildred Welsher, Gordon Voss, Clifford Symes, Arthur Sully, Barbara Lamming, Margaret Lamming, Lily Sweetland, Victor Groves, Vera Yandle, Vera Morse, Doris Fowler, Amelia Eslick, Patricia White, Gerald Grandfield, Joan Gooding, Leslie Sweetland, Frederick Eslick, Sidney Moles, Margaret Voss, Betty Davey.

Chapter 4
Mothers' Union in the Three Parishes

The Mothers' Union is a worldwide Anglican organisation founded in 1876 by Mary Sumner. Its objectives are to uphold the sanctity of marriage, the family, to promote conditions in society favourable to family life and the protection of children. The first mention of the Mothers' Union in the Bath and Wells Diocese is made in 1894.

The Dunster Deanery, of which Bicknoller and Sampford Brett were part, had a representative in 1902, and in 1904 the Taunton Archdeaconry representative was the Honourable Mrs Ethel Trollope, of Crowcombe Court.

A new branch at Sampford Brett was formed in 1910 with 20 members, including the branch secretary Mrs Foster, of the Rectory. The Bicknoller branch began in 1912 and the records show that Mrs Couch, of the Rectory, was the Enrolling Member until 1927, being succeeded by Mrs Harman in 1928.

The early history of Crowcombe Mothers' Union is vague, but a branch is listed in 1911, although the handbooks are missing. In 1908 the Honourable Mrs Trollope opened a branch at Watchet and is mentioned as still encouraging new branches in the district in 1918. Mrs Howes was the secretary for Crowcombe in 1930 and work began on their banner in the mid-1930s, with every member setting some stitches and being involved in its making. However, the banner was sent to professional embroiderers for the insertion of the 'Blessed Virgin Mary and Child' figures. Often invitations were extended to Bicknoller and Sampford Brett branches to attend meetings at Crowcombe. A regular visitor at such meetings was Mrs Rose Luttrell, who for several years served as Deanery literature secretary.

On the Lady Day Festival in 1933 Mrs Rosa Ellen Baker, of Timewell Cottage, Crowcombe, and her daughter, Mrs Queenie Payne, who lived at Halsway, were enrolled. Mrs Payne later moved to Sampford Brett and so transferred to that branch. In 1993 Mrs Payne received a long service certificate for 60 years' membership.

Mrs Ethel Welsher, of Crowcombe, was enrolled in 1948 and at the time of writing is still a member of the Quantock Towers Branch in the Quantock Deanery.

Mrs Molly Farmer, of Bicknoller, was the Taunton Archdeaconry president from 1995–97 and is now Secretary of the Quantock Tower Branch which is run by a committee.

In 1998 Mrs Farmer was succeeded as Taunton Archdeaconry president by another member of the branch, Mrs Jeanette Bole, wife of the then rector, the Revd Malcolm Bole. After serving for three years in this office, Mrs Bole was elected Bath and Wells Diocesan president, the highest attainment, to date, of any branch member, and one which she held for the triennial, 2001–03.

Members of the Bicknoller branch of the Mothers' Union in Guatamalan costume to celebrate the Women's World Day of Prayer, 1993. Left to right: Pat Wheeler, Elizabeth Darke, Mary Gadd, Dorothy Brown, Molly Farmer, Maureen Canney.

Some members of the Quantock Towers Benefice Mothers' Union with their new banner. Left to right, standing: Rosalie (Rose) Fish, Maureen Canney, Mary Gadd; seated: Dorothy Royston, Nancy Price, Gillian Southwood, Ken Canney, Ethel Welsher.

Four members of the Bicknoller, Crowcombe and Sampford Brett branch of the Mothers' Union. Left to right: Ethel Welsher, Mary Rudram, Wendy Venner, Rosalie (Rose) Fish.

Subscribers

Mrs Edna F.M. Alison (née Jewell), Wembdon, Somerset
Susan Appleby, Bicknoller, Somerset
Peter and Betty Armstrong, Trull, Taunton
Linda and Martin Barnes, Minehead
The Barrett Family, Kilnridge, Sampford Brett
Gwyn Bennett, West Quantoxhead
The Billinge Family, Crowcombe
Ann and Keith Bishop, Williton, Somerset
Martin and Liz Blazey, Sampford Brett
Richard Boddington, Crowcombe, Somerset
John and Yvonne Bonser, Blue Anchor, Somerset
Chris Boyles, Alcombe, Minehead, Somerset
Christopher V. Brewer, Crowcombe, Somerset
V.A. Brewer, Crowcombe
David Bulpin, Williton, Somerset
Joe and Rita Butterworth, Crowcombe, Somerset
Annabel M. Campbell, Sampford Brett
Mr K.W. and Mrs J. Carter, Sampford Brett
Mike and Wendy Chapman, Yeovil, Somerset
Mrs M.R. Chester
Maurice and Joyce Chidgey, Watchet, Somerset
Vera Chidgey, Williton, Somerset
Rev C.R.B. and Mrs Coleman, Hunstanton, Norfolk
J. Rosemary Cox M.B.E., Willett, Somerset
The Darke Family, Bicknoller, Somerset
Denis and Hazel Davis, Minehead, Somerset
Raymond Davis, Colchester, Essex
Annette and Samuel Dickinson and Lee Graham, Exeter, Devon
Keith Dickinson
Richard Dinwiddy, Ruishton, Taunton
June and Jeffrey Duddridge, Crowcombe, Somerset
Paul and Mary Duddridge, Stogumber, Somerset
M. and G. Dunn, Lawford, Crowcombe
Audrey and David Emery, Sampford Brett
Keith and Molly Farmer, Bicknoller
Robert and Wendy Farmer, Bicknoller and Edinburgh
Ray Fisher, Bicknoller, Somerset
Drs David and Shirley Gover, Bicknoller, Somerset
Leonard Groves, formerly of Sampford Brett
Mr Stephen Ridd Groves and Mrs Janet E. Groves, Watchet, Somerset
George and Patricia Haller, Crowcombe, Somerset
Hayes, Crowcombe, Somerset
Jack Henson, Slowley Bungalow, Luxborough, Watchet
Roland and Lorna Hobbs, Bicknoller, Somerset
Steve and Sam Hobbs, Bicknoller, Somerset
Joan Hugan, U.S.A.
Louise Jeffreys, Bicknoller
David and Margaret Jenkins, Crowcombe, Somerset
John and Lorna Jenkins, Alcombe, Minehead, Somerset
Mrs Barbara Jewell (née Criddle), Taunton, Somerset
Daphne M. Jones, Taunton, Somerset
Christine and Peter King, Sampford Brett
Brenda Knight, Sampford Brett, Somerset
Dennis and Joan Knight, Bromley, Kent
Mr and Mrs B.H. Langley, Watermead
Georgina Langley, Willett, Somerset
Chris and Ann Leigh, Bicknoller, Somerset
Christopher J. Lewis, Crowcombe, Somerset
Norah G. Linck
Eileen and Brian Lloyd, Bicknoller
Mrs S.A. Looker, Milverton, Somerset
Miss Audrey Lyddon, Bicknoller
Russell Philip Besley Lyddon, Paignton, Devon

Mrs Mary E. Maine, Bicknoller, Somerset
Mr and Mrs Paul Mansfield, Cardiff
Allan and Gwen Marks, Crowcombe Heathfield, Somerset
Peter and Valori Menneer, Crowcombe
Marie Breley Milnes (née Gadd), Williton, Somerset
The Mowat Family, Crowcombe, Somerset
Kathleen M. Mullins (linked with Jennings family), South Petherton, Somerset
Robin and Patricia Murchie, Crowcombe
Nick and Jackie Nation, Lydeard St Lawrence, Taunton
Sue and Mark Ogden, Bicknoller, Somerset
Mrs Vera Pearse (née Merson), Wellington, Somerset
Kevin and Catherine Pickin (née Farmer), Bicknoller and Ladbroke, Warwickshire
Leslie Pike, Brewers Water Farm, Crowcombe
Stephen, Lisa, Ethan and Ebony Plenty, Alcombe, Minehead, Somerset
Stanley Powe (In Memory of), Crowcombe, Somerset
John and Lesley Procter, Sampford Brett, Somerset
Rob and Margaret Reed, Sampford Brett
Mrs Mary Rhodes, Watchet, Somerset
Jane and Edward Rhys, Alderley, Gloucestershire
Valerie Richards, Torweston Farm
Christopher Rutt, Bicknoller, Somerset
David Rutt, Bicknoller, Somerset
Mr R.C. Saunders, Crowcombe, Somerset
Jane and Ian Sefton
K. Joyce Setter, Taunton, Somerset
C.P. Sharp OBE, Maulden, Bedfordshire
Molly Singerton-Cole, Midsomer Norton, Bath
B. and J. Skudder, Doniford
Martin and Gill Southwood, Bicknoller
Peter and Peggy Stradling, Sampford Brett, Somerset
Mr D.W., MBE, and Mrs S.A. Sully, Williton
Phil and Jan Swan, Sampford Brett
Carol and David Thorpe
Sheila M. Timson, Sampford Brett, Somerset
Keith and Joy Towells, Watchet
Julia M. Tremlett, Bicknoller, Somerset
Jillian M. Trethewey, Glen Waverley, Victoria, Australia
Clifford E. Trickey, Bicknoller, Somerset
Daphne and Anthony Trollope-Bellew
Anthony Trollope-Bellew, Crowcombe
John F.W. Walling, Newton Abbot, Devon
Alastair and Cameron Weldon, Sampford Brett, Somerset
Jane Wheeler (née Farmer), Bicknoller and Minehead
Peter M. White, formerly of Williton, Somerset
Ralph and Brenda White, Liddimore Farm, Watchet
Heather and Mark Wilson, Lawford
Mrs Doreen M. Woodward, Williton, Somerset
R.J., V.A., and D.J. Yandle, Sampford Brett

FURTHER TITLES

Community Histories

The Book of Addiscombe • Canning and Clyde Road Residents Association and Friends
The Book of Addiscombe, Vol. II • Canning and Clyde Road Residents Association and Friends
The Book of Ashburton • Stuart Hands and Pete Webb
The Book of Axminster with Kilmington • Les Berry and Gerald Gosling
Bakewell • Trevor Brighton
The Book of Bampton • Caroline Seward
The Book of Barnstaple • Avril Stone
The Book of Barnstaple, Vol. II • Avril Stone
The Book of The Bedwyns • Bedwyn History Society
The Book of Bergh Apton • Geoffrey I. Kelly
The Book of Bickington • Stuart Hands
The Book of Bideford • Peter Christie and Alison Grant
Blandford Forum: A Millennium Portrait • Blandford Forum Town Council
The Book of Boscastle • Rod and Anne Knight
The Book of Bourton-on-the-Hill, Batsford and Sezincote • Allen Firth
The Book of Bramford • Bramford Local History Group
The Book of Breage & Germoe • Stephen Polglase
The Book of Bridestowe • D. Richard Cann
The Book of Bridport • Rodney Legg
The Book of Brixham • Frank Pearce
The Book of Buckfastleigh • Sandra Coleman
The Book of Buckland Monachorum & Yelverton • Pauline Hamilton-Leggett
The Book of Budleigh Salterton • D. Richard Cann
The Book of Carharrack • Carharrack Old Cornwall Society
The Book of Carshalton • Stella Wilks and Gordon Rookledge
The Parish Book of Cerne Abbas • Vivian and Patricia Vale
The Book of Chagford • Iain Rice
The Book of Chapel-en-le-Frith • Mike Smith
The Book of Chittlehamholt with Warkleigh & Satterleigh • Richard Lethbridge
The Book of Chittlehampton • Various
The Book of Codford • Romy Wyeth
The Book of Colney Heath • Bryan Lilley
The Book of Constantine • Moore and Trethowan
The Book of Cornwood and Lutton • Compiled by the People of the Parish
The Book of Crediton • John Heal
The Book of Creech St Michael • June Small
The Book of Crowcombe, Bicknoller and Sampford Brett • Maurice and Joyce Chidgey
The Book of Crudwell • Tony Pain
The Book of Cullompton • Compiled by the People of the Parish
The Book of Dawlish • Frank Pearce
The Book of Dulverton, Brushford, Bury & Exebridge • Dulverton and District Civic Society
The Book of Dunster • Hilary Binding
The Book of Easton • Easton Village History Project
The Book of Edale • Gordon Miller
The Ellacombe Book • Sydney R. Langmead
The Book of Exmouth • W.H. Pascoe
The Book of Grampound with Creed • Bane and Oliver
The Book of Gosport • Lesley Burton and Brian Musselwhite
The Book of Haughley • Howard Stephens
The Book of Hayle • Harry Pascoe
The Book of Hayling Island & Langstone • Peter Rogers
The Book of Helston • Jenkin with Carter
The Book of Hemyock • Clist and Dracott
The Book of Herne Hill • Patricia Jenkyns
The Book of Hethersett • Hethersett Society Research Group
The Book of High Bickington • Avril Stone
The Book of Honiton • Gerald Gosling
The Book of Ilsington • Dick Wills
The Book of Kingskerswell • Carsewella Local History Group
The Book of Lamerton • Ann Cole and Friends
Lanner, A Cornish Mining Parish • Sharron Schwartz and Roger Parker
The Book of Leigh & Bransford • Malcolm Scott
The Second Book of Leigh & Bransford • Malcolm Scott
The Book of Litcham with Lexham & Mileham • Litcham Historical and Amenity Society
The Book of Llangain • Haydyn Williams
The Book of Loddiswell • Loddiswell Parish History Group
The New Book of Lostwithiel • Barbara Fraser
The Book of Lulworth • Rodney Legg
The Book of Lustleigh • Joe Crowdy
The Book of Lydford • Compiled by Barbara Weeks
The Book of Lyme Regis • Rodney Legg
The Book of Manaton • Compiled by the People of the Parish

The Book of Markyate • Markyate Local History Society
The Book of Mawnan • Mawnan Local History Group
The Book of Meavy • Pauline Hemery
The Book of Mere • Dr David Longbourne
The Book of Minehead with Alcombe • Binding and Stevens
The Book of Monks Orchard and Eden Park • Ian Muir and Pat Manning
The Book of Morchard Bishop • Jeff Kingaby
The Book of Mylor • Mylor Local History Group
The Book of Narborough • Narborough Local History Society
The Book of Newdigate • John Callcut
The Book of Newtown • Keir Foss
The Book of Nidderdale • Nidderdale Museum Society
The Book of Northlew with Ashbury • Northlew History Group
The Book of North Newton • J.C. and K.C. Robins
The Book of North Tawton • Baker, Hoare and Shields
The Book of Nynehead • Nynehead & District History Society
The Book of Okehampton • Roy and Ursula Radford
The Book of Ottery St Mary • Gerald Gosling and Peter Harris
The Book of Paignton • Frank Pearce
The Book of Penge, Anerley & Crystal Palace • Peter Abbott
The Book of Peter Tavy with Cudlipptown • Peter Tavy Heritage Group
The Book of Pimperne • Jean Coull
The Book of Plymtree • Tony Eames
The Book of Poole • Rodney Legg
The Book of Porlock • Dennis Corner
Postbridge – The Heart of Dartmoor • Reg Bellamy
The Book of Priddy • Albert Thompson
The Book of Princetown • Dr Gardner-Thorpe
The Book of Probus • Alan Kent and Danny Merrifield
The Book of Rattery • By the People of the Parish
The Book of Roadwater, Leighland and Treborough • Clare and Glyn Court
The Book of St Austell • Peter Hancock
The Book of St Day • Joseph Mills and Paul Annear
The Book of St Dennis and Goss Moor • Kenneth Rickard
The Book of St Levan • St Levan Local History Group
The Book of Sampford Courtenay with Honeychurch • Stephanie Pouya
The Book of Sculthorpe • Gary Windeler
The Book of Seaton • Ted Gosling
The Book of Sidmouth • Ted Gosling and Sheila Luxton
The Book of Silverton • Silverton Local History Society
The Book of South Molton • Jonathan Edmunds
The Book of South Stoke with Midford • Edited by Robert Parfitt
South Tawton & South Zeal with Sticklepath • Roy and Ursula Radford
The Book of Sparkwell with Hemerdon & Lee Mill • Pam James
The Book of Staverton • Pete Lavis
The Book of Stithians • Stithians Parish History Group
The Book of Stogumber, Monksilver, Nettlecombe & Elworthy • Maurice and Joyce Chidgey
The Book of South Brent • Greg Wall
The Book of Studland • Rodney Legg
The Book of Swanage • Rodney Legg
The Book of Tavistock • Gerry Woodcock
The Book of Thorley • Sylvia McDonald and Bill Hardy
The Book of Torbay • Frank Pearce
The Book of Truro • Christine Parnell
The Book of Uplyme • Gerald Gosling and Jack Thomas
The Book of Watchet • Compiled by David Banks
The Book of Wendling, Longham and Beeston with Bittering • Stephen Olley
The Book of West Huntspill • By the People of the Parish
The Book of Weston-super-Mare • Sharon Poole
The Book of Whitchurch • Gerry Woodcock
Widecombe-in-the-Moor • Stephen Woods
Widecombe – Uncle Tom Cobley & All • Stephen Woods
The Book of Williton • Michael Williams
The Book of Wincanton • Rodney Legg
The Book of Winscombe • Margaret Tucker
The Book of Witheridge • Peter and Freda Tout and John Usmar
The Book of Withycombe • Chris Boyles
Woodbury: The Twentieth Century Revisited • Roger Stokes
The Book of Woolmer Green • Compiled by the People of the Parish
The Book of Yetminster • Shelagh Hill

For details of any of the above titles or if you are interested in writing your own history, please contact: Commissioning Editor, Community Histories, Halsgrove House, Lower Moor Way, Tiverton, Devon EX16 6SS, England; email: katyc@halsgrove.com